BATTLE OVER THE THIRD REICH
The Air War Over Germany 1943/45

Werner Held

Werner Held

BATTLE OVER THE THIRD REICH

The Air War Over Germany 1943/1945

AIR RESEARCH PUBLICATIONS

First published 1988 by
Podzun-Pallas—Verlag GMBH
Markt 9, 6360 Friedburg 3
Dorheim, West Germany.
© 1988 Podzun-Pallas.

English edition published 1990 by
Air Research Publications
34 Elm Road, New Malden
Surrey, KT3 3HD
Great Britain.
© 1990 Air Research

All rights reserved. No part of
this publication may be
reproduced, stored in a
retrieval system, or transmitted
in any form or by any means
without prior permission in
writing from the publisher.
ISBN 1 871187 10 9

English language typesetting by
Qualitext, Andover, Hants. Tel: 334220
Printed and bound in Great Britain by
L R Printing Services Ltd.
Burgess Hill, Sussex RH15 9UA.

Contents

Foreword	7
A Word of Thanks	8
The Military Position in Late 1942	9
1943	9
1944	11
1945	13
Bibliography	16
The Photographs	17
Index	184

Foreword

The chapter in the Luftwaffe's history in which it fought to defend Germany against the ever increasing weight of British and American air attack is known as 'Reichsverteidigung'. It was a time of heroism and of sacrifice, for the German fighter pilots knew full well that they were fighting to defend their own homeland and their families from the death and destruction which was being wrought on an unparalleled scale by the Allied bombers.

Just as the fighter pilots of the Royal Air Force gave their all in the Battle of Britain in 1940, the young men of the Luftwaffe now laid down their lives in the defence of their country.

Assemblying the collection of photographs which would do justice to the subject was a task which occupied me for many years. The published material available on the subject of *Reichsverteidigung* 1943–45 is sparse indeed. The reason that this has remained so for so many years is that much of the photographic material exists only in the personal albums of the participants, or with their relatives. The key to unlocking this treasure-trove of memories is not one that is given up easily and it is only through the good will of many that I have been able make use of their private collections.

Special thanks must go to the members of the *Gemeinschaft der Jagdflieger* (the Association of Fighter Pilots) who provided such vital help via their organisation and their publication *Jägerblatt*.

Despite the lengths gone to ensure that a full and balanced account is given, it has not been possible to cover ever aspect in the detail some may wish. There are many areas where practically no photographic material has survived the long years since the end of World War II, and still others where only a few fragmentary glimpses are afforded through the snap shots taken by the pilots themselves. Although great strides in the development of weapons systems were made during the war, I have chosen to concentrate upon the men, their achievements and sacrifices.

I hope to have provided a worthy tribute to the sacrifice of the thousands of young men from many countries, and even continents, that fought in the skies over Germany.

Koblenz, summer 1988   Werner Held

A Word of Thanks

The battle for the Third Reich was a time of heartbreak and tragedy for the Luftwaffe's fighter force, as well as its ultimate test. In this book I have tried to illustrate the deeds of these testing years before they are absorbed in the ever thickening mists of time. I can only hope that I have been successful in this, and if I have then the credit is largely due to my friends who put the material at my disposal.

I thank my friends:

Gebhard Aders
Hans-Ekkehard Bob
Manfred Boehme
Hermann Buchner
Kurt Bühligen +
Georg Christl
Walter Dahl +
Urban L. Drew
Georg-Peter Eder +
Albrecht Fuest
Adolf Galland
Horst Geyer
Rolf Glogner
Hermann Graf
Helmut Haugk
Heinz Knoke
Helmut Lennartz

Fritz Losigkeit
Rudolf Nowotny
Ernst Obermajer
Robert Olejnik
Albert Palm
Peter Petrick
Hermann Riedel
Ossi Romm
Hans Rossbach
Ernst Schröder
Leo Schuhmacher
Rudolf Sinner
Gerhard Stamp
H. H. Stapfer
Frau Sigrid Tank
Erich Warsitz +

The military position in late 1942

The tide of the battles on the Eastern Front and in the North African Theatre had already begun to turn against Germany:

RUSSIA

November 23rd, 1942. Russian forces had surrounded the German 6th Army in Stalingrad.
December 23rd, 1942. Operation Wintergewitter (Winter Storm) to free the 6th Army, failed and the fate of the beseiged units was finally sealed.
February 3rd, 1943. Generalfeldmarschall Paulus surrendered the 6th Army at Stalingrad. Bomber, fighter and special transport units attempting to airlift supplies to the army had been sacrificed in vain.

NORTH AFRICA

October 23rd, 1942. Second Battle of El Alamein, major offensive by the British 8th Army pushes the Axis forces back to Tunisia.
November 8th, 1942. Operation Torch, Allied landings in North Africa, signal a quick end to Rommel's Army.
May 13th, 1943. General von Arnim surrenders Axis forces. 252,000 German troops captured.
With the end of the North African campaign, the Allies begin to turn their attentions towards Fortress Europe and the heartland of the Third Reich.
The outcome of the conference between Churchill and Roosevelt at Casablanca in January, 1943, marks the beginning of the end for Germany. At this time a plan for the air war against Germany was being formulated under which American planes would bomb by day and British by night. From now on Germany's towns and cities would become the targets for the largest bomber force ever assembled. 'Casablanca', Air Marshal Harris said, 'removed the last moral barrier to the total bombing war'.

1943

January 27th, 1943. 55 American B-17 bombers escorted by P-38 fighters attacked military targets at Wilhelmshaven by day. Three B-17s are brought down by fighters of JG1. This small attack was a prelude to the maximum effort raids which, by the war's end would launch up to 3,000 aircraft a day at Germany
The defence against the American bombers in early 1943 lay with three Jagdgeschwadern (fighter wings) JG1, JG2 and JG26. The

remaining fighter units were fully committed to the Russian and North African Fronts. At this early stage American escort fighters lacked the range to accompany the bombers of the U.S. Army Air Force far over German occupied Europe and the bomber crews relied solely upon their defensive armament for protection.

To develop effective weapons to combat this new phenomenon of large, heavily armed formations Erprobungskommando 20 was established at Wittmundhafen and later moved to Achmer, near Osnabrück. Amongst the weapons developed here were 21 cm rockets which could be launched from under the wings of fighters out of range of the bomber's defensive fire.

In April 1943 the fighters in the west were reinforced by the formation of JG11 in Northern Germany. The fighter pilots began to achieve some good results, but had to pay a high price for their success.

In May 1943 the U.S. 8th Air force transferred 300 four engined bombers from North Africa to Britain. The RAF continued their night attacks on the German armament industry in major towns in northern Germany and the Ruhr, whilst the Americans made daylight attacks on north, central and southern Germany.

92 B-17s attacked the Continental rubber works in Hanover on July 26th, 1943. Sixteen bombers were shot down for the loss of five fighters. On July 28th, a series of heavy attacks against the German aircraft industry began. During the first mission to Kassel and Oschersleben JG11 brought down eleven of the fifteen bombers lost, but on July 30th, in another attack on Kassel, 23 fighters were lost and 12 of the bombers brought down. 53 B-24 Liberators were lost in the attack on oil installations at Ploesti in Rumania on August 1st, 1943. Still more crash landed on their return to Libya, only 33 of the 178 bombers remaining air worthy. On August 17th, the ball bearing plants at Schweinfurt became the target for 230 B-17 crews, 36 were brought down. In another attack on the same day, against the Messerschmitt factory at Regensburg, 24 out of the 147 bombers were lost. 17 Luftwaffe fighter pilots were killed on this day.

The number of aircraft taking part in the raids continued to increase and no less than 1,462 heavy bombers took part in raids on Kiel, Bremen and Hamburg on December 13th. Only 16 bombers were lost, due partly to the choice of targets and that the P-51 Mustang escort fighter was used on a large scale for the first time.

More Luftwaffe fighter units were diverted to assist in the Reichsverteidigung in 1943.
III/JG54 in March.
Jagdgruppe 25 from August to December.
JG3 in August.
III/JG77 in August to protect the Rumanian oil fields.

II/JG53 in November to reinforce the Vienna sector.
JG300 *Wilde Sau* at the end of the year.
JG301 and JG302 forming late in the year.
III/ZG26 in the summer.
II/ZG26 formed from III/ZG1 and III/ZG26.
ZG76 reformed in August to use the Me 410.

1944

1944 was the year in which the Luftwaffe fighter force's back was broken by sheer weight of numbers. It was a year of great sacrifice and many of the finest pilots lost their lives in the battle to defend their country. Experience and courage proved not to be enough when facing overwhelming odds.

The first American attacks came on January 11th. 26 Luftwaffe pilots were killed, but 44 of the 487 attacking aircraft were brought down. A still larger attack was made on January 29th, when Frankfurt am Main and Ludwigshafen were the targets. 29 of the 863 bombers attacking were shot down, the Luftwaffe lost 25 pilots with a further 30 injured.

Then came 'Big Week'. Between February 20th and 25th the Americans lost 154 bombers. Day fighter, *Zerstörer* and night fighter units fought some savage battles and lost 99 pilots, another 66 being wounded.

The combined RAF and American bombing campaign against Germany was now reaching its climax. The first large scale daylight raid against Berlin was made on March 6th. A total of 69 bombers were lost on this and other targets attacked during the day, 30 Luftwaffe pilots were killed.

The massive fighter escort of P-51s now had the range to accompany the bombers deep into Germany. This meant increasingly heavy losses for the defending fighters, especially for the *Zerstörer* units. On February 22nd, II/ZG26 based at Nordhausen/Harz lost their commander and leading exponent of the twin engined fighter, Hauptmann Tratt. On March 16th, ZG76 intercepted a large raid near Augsburg, twelve men were killed and twelve more injured.

In April the attacks on Germany reached their peak. In 18 days 554 Allied aircraft were brought down and 122 severely damaged. The Luftwaffe suffered 209 pilots killed, 61 missing and 125 wounded. Despite the disruption to German industry caused by the Allied attacks, aircraft production reached its peak during 1944 under the leadership of Albert Speer and Dipl. Ing. Karl Otto Saur. Through de-centralisation and dispersal of factories, the use of underground plants and bomb-proof shelters production of fighters rose from 1,323 in February to 3,535 in September 1944.

As the production of fighters increased, so must the output of trained pilots. The training units worked hard, but there was no time to turn young men into experienced fighter pilots. Many a young pilot was sent into combat too soon and payed with his life — the air over the Reich was an unforgiving class room.

Despite the Allied bombing the Luftwaffe was able to develop some very advanced ideas. The Me 262 jet fighter could have been a tremendous boost to the German fighter units, but Hitler insisted that priority should be given to a ground attack version which could be used against invading armies. The Me 262 might also have been able to counter the P-51 Mustang long range fighter which was becoming a crippling thorn in the Luftwaffe's side. Only in the final months of the war was Kommando Nowotny and JG7 able to use the new jet to its full, but by then it was far too late to have any bearing upon the outcome.

Another remarkable aircraft was the diminutive Me 163 'Komet' rocket fighter. Powered by a liquid fuel rocket motor, the Me 163 had a fantastic performance, but strictly limited endurance. In the final analysis it was more spectacular then deadly. Only nine Allied aircraft are known to have been shot down by Me 163s, but far more pilots were killed attempting to fly it.

The Do 335 took another and unique approach to pushing forward the limits of performance. Using two engines in the fuselage, driving propellers for and aft, it became the fastest piston engined aircraft of the war, but it never entered combat. Still more types were under development when the war ended, the FW Ta 152, FW 190D-9, He 162 and many others.

Attacks on German oil production and refining capacity began in earnest in April, 1944, and began to bring all transport to a grinding halt. Massed bomber formation continued to batter an already devastated Germany in the defence of which only a token resistance could be mounted. Escort fighters were now increasingly freed from their charges and sent marauding over what was left of the Reich, strafing anything that moved, and quite a few things which did not. Scores of aircraft were destroyed on their airfields and those that did manage to leave the ground were as often as not shot down on take off or landing, their most vulnerable time even for the jets. Now even the most experienced fighter pilot was helpless.

On June 21st, 1,234 bombers and 1,269 fighters operated over Germany, many going to Berlin. 145 B-17s bombed the hydroelectric power station at Ruhland and carried on to land at Poltava in Russia, where an attempt was made to destroy them by Luftwaffe bomber units.

Throughout July, August and September the heavy air attacks continued and to counter this came the *Sturmgruppen*. These Storm Groups were charged with the task of breaking through the defending fighter escort and pressing home their attacks on the bombers. To help the *Sturm* pilots their aircraft were given extra armoured plate for protection and other conventional fighter units were assigned to stave off the Mustangs and Thunderbolts, leaving them free to attack the bombers. The tactic worked, up to a point, but it required a particularly courageous pilot, whose career was often spectacular, and short.

1945

The losses being suffered by the Luftwaffe were becoming unacceptably high, but there was no option but to continue fighting until Germany surrendered. A last hope came in the shape of the Ardennes counter offensive and, on January 1st, Operation Bodenplatte, in which many Allied aircraft were destroyed on the ground.

The situation was now rapidly becoming even worse for the Third Reich. In the west the Allied armies were nearing the Rhine, in the east the Russian offensive was pushing the German army back and in the south Allied forces were pushing northwards through Italy.

In February many fighter units were moved from Reichsverteidigung duties to the eastern front in a desperate attempt to slow the Russian advance. A decision had been taken to leave German cities open to attack rather than see the Russians mercilessly push deep into the Reich.

German railways and communications were continually disrupted by air attack. The end was now in sight, RAF and American aircraft could roam Germany almost without risk of interception, they had at last achieved total air superiority. The Reich lay in ruins, its cities reduced to rubble, its industry to ashes. Out of woodland airstrips and from Autobahns the last remaining fighters continued to fly, the losses of men and machines in these last days were not even recorded. It is certain that casualties were high, it is even known for pilots to be shot whilst descending in their parachutes.

In February III/JG7 began operations with Me 262s. On the 22nd, 34 Me 262s took off, five pilots engaged and claimed aircraft shot down, three jets were lost. In March JG7 flew the largest jet fighter operations of the war and on the 18th used the R4M rockets for the first time. On March 31st, a new unit, Jagdverband 44, moved to München/Reim to begin operations. JV44 was led by the now disgraced General der Jagdflieger Adolf Galland and had amongst its number more experienced and highly decorated pilots than any other unit. Oberst Lützow accepted demotion to Unteroffizier so that he could join JV44 which was nicknamed the Ritterkreuz Geschwader.

Over the Reich the last few pilots continued to fly against overwhelming odds. The last successful battle was fought on March 18th, when around 1,200 bombers escorted by over 400 fighters attacked Berlin. 13 bombers and six fighters were shot down. The last air battle over Germany was fought on April 7th, between Sonderkommando Elbe and 2,000 aircraft of the 8th Air Force. The pilots of Sonderkommando Elbe were instructed to make a diving attack on a bomber, firing all the way, and if the enemy had not been shot down they were to ram. Six of the 17 bombers lost are known to have been rammed, German figures show that 77 pilots of this last ditch unit were lost.

April 25th. Russian and American troops met on the River Elbe.

April 26th. Berlin was encircled by the Russians.

April 29th. 1,000,000 German troops surrendered in Northern Italy and Austria.

April 30th. Adolf Hitler committed suicide.

At midnight on May 9th, troops on all fronts laid down their arms. The war in Europe had come to an end.

Bibliography

Manfred Boehme: "Jagdgeschwader 7", Motorbuch-Verlag, Stuttgart.
Heinz Conradis: "Forschen und Fliegen", Musterschmidt-Verlag, Göttingen.
Walter Dahl: "Rammjäger" Heimreiter-Verlag, Heusenstamm.
I. L. Ethel: "Komet", Motorbuch-Verlag, Stuttgart.
Adolf Galland: "The First and the Last", Verlag Schneekluth, München.
Werner Held: "Adolf Galland", Podzun-Pallas-Verlag, Dorheim.
Werner Held: "Die Deutsche Tagjagd" Motorbuch-Verlag, Stuttgart.
Werner Held: "Walter Nowotny", Motorbuch-Verlag, Stuttgart.
Heinz Knoke: "Die Grosse Jagd", Verlag C. Bösendahl, Rinteln.
Ernst Obermaier: "Die Ritterkreuzträger der Luftwaffe I, 1939/45" Verlag D. Hoffmann, Mainz.
Josef Priller "JG26 — Geschichte eines Jagdgeschwaders", Verlag Vowinkel, Heidelberg.
Wolfgang Wagner: "Kurt Tank", Verlag Bernard u. Graefe, Munich.
Mano Ziegler: "Me 262", Motorbuch-Verlag, Stuttgart.
"Jagerblatt" — The official publication of the Gemeinschaft der Jagdflieger.
William Green: "Warplanes of the Third Reich", Doubleday, New York.
Uwe Feist: "The Fighting Me 109" Arms and Armour Press, London.
R. Freeman: "Mighty Eighth War Diary", Jane's, London.
Smith & Kay: "German Aircraft of the Second World War", Putnam, London.
C. Bishop: "Fortresses of the Big Triangle First", East Anglia Books, Bishop's Stortford, England.
Bernd Barbas: "Planes of the Luftwaffe Fighter Aces", Kookaburra, Melbourne, Australia.

Glossary

Zerstörer (Destroyer) Luftwaffe terminology for a heavy fighter, usually Me 110 or Me 410. The majority of the aircraft were used by *Zerstörer* Geschwadern, Such as ZG26

Sturm (Storm) *Sturmstaffel* and *Sturmgruppe*. Specialist units established within *Jagdgeschwadern* (fighter wings) to attack heavy bomber formations. Their aircraft were often equipped with extra armour for protection against return fire.

Viermot (Four engine) The generic term for 4 engined bombers, mainly B-17s and B-24s. As the destruction of a *Viermot* was seen as an achievement greater than the destruction of other aircraft, the number of *Viermot* destroyed by a pilot was often counted separately.

Ritterkreuz (Knight's Cross of the Iron Cross) The highest award of the Third Reich, awarded for outstanding bravery in the face of the enemy. Should a man warrant further commendation he would receive ribbon clasps; Oak Leaves (101); Oak Leaves and Swords (25); Oak Leaves, Swords and Diamonds (9). Figures in brackets are the total numbers of the awards presented to Luftwaffe fighter pilots.

Jadgeschwader 2 was in the front line, facing Britain from the west coast of Europe and the first line of defence against Allied raids. Geschwader Kommodore in 1942 was 29 year old Oberstleutnant Walter Oesau, a veteran of the Spanish Campaign. He received the Ritterkreuz in August 1940, the Oak Leaves in February 1941 and Swords to the Ritterkreuz on July 15th, 1941.

'Ace of the West' Hauptmann Egon Mayer, Kommandeur of III Gruppe JG2 from November '42 until promoted to Kommodore of JG2 in July '43. On February 2nd, 1944, he became the first pilot to achieve 100 victories on the Channel Front.

Mayer (second from the left) briefs his men for another sortie.

17

IV/JG1 operated over Northern Germany, Holland, Denmark and Southern Norway. This devil emblem was adopted by the Gruppe in the spring of 1942.

Hauptmann Fritz Losigkeit, Kommandeur of IV/JG1. Losigkeit became Gruppen Kommandeur on his return from a diplomatic mission to Japan and finished the war on the Russian Front as Kommodore of JG77.

II/JG1, based in Northern Holland, became the first operational FW 190 Gruppe. These machines are from the 4th Staffel JG1, commanded by 31 year old Oberleutnant Robert Olejnik. The *Tatzelwurm* emblem was often used on JG1s machines.

The original caption to this American photo' was, 'Why it's bad luck to fool with a Fortress', and shows the defensive armament.

P-38 Lightnings acted as fighter escort to the Fortresses on these early raids.

The aptly named Flying Fortress could put up a formidable return fire. Here an Obergefreiter looks into the 'Business End' of a captured B-17F 42-3190 which force landed at Anthony-sur-Seine on July 14th, 1943. This was formally Captain Kee H. Harrison's 94th Bomb Group machine.

The characteristic bumps on an Me 109G of 1/JG1.

Top a *Rotte* (pair) from 2/JG1. They are flown by Leutnant Knoke and Unteroffizier Wolf (below) in search of high flying Mosquito reconnaissance machines. Albin Wolf became a top scoring pilot with JG54 *Grünherz* (Green Heart) on the Russian Front. He was killed on April 2nd, 1944, after claiming the destruction of 144 aircraft.

Carried high on the shoulders of his comrades, Oberleutnant Framm of IV/JG1 celebrates the destruction of one of the elusive reconnaissance aircraft at Munchen-Gladbach.

The clearly visible contrails of the high flying American formations acted as clear sign posts for the fighter pilots.

A B-17 of the 94th Bomb Group finds its final resting place.

21

FW 190s of 8/JG26 in close formation.

An FW 190 of II/JG2 taxies out for a sortie over the Cherbourg–Le Havre area.

All three Gruppen of JG26 were based on the Channel Front, charged with patrolling the area from Normandy to the Schelde Estuary. Major Schöpfel (centre) led the Geschwader from January 10th, 1943. I/JG26 came under the command of 28 year old Hauptmann Johannes Seifert (left) in January '43.

I/JG1 under the command of Hauptmann Beise, at Jever. These Me 109 'Gustavs' are at 30 minute readiness.

Leutnant Steiger returns after a patrol in February '43. Left is Leutnant Gerhard and right is Unteroffizier Raddatz.

A few days later Steiger was killed and laid to rest amidst much ceremony near I/J1s base at Jever.

When beyond the range of escort fighters the Luftwaffe used Me 110 *Zerstörer* (Destroyers) against the bomber formations.

By 1943 the majority of Me 110s were employed as night fighters, but they were often pressed into service in daylight. On February 26th, 1943, 32 year old Hauptmann Ludwig Becker, holder of the Ritterkreuz with Oak Leaves and Staffelkapitän of 12/NJG1, failed to return from a daylight sortie over the North Sea. His radio operator, Oberfeldwebel Staub, who had participated in 40 of Beckers 46 night victories, was lost with him.

Another holder of the Oak Leaves was 24 year old Hauptmann Friedrich Geisshardt. After fighting in Poland, the Battle of Britain, Russia and North Africa he had over 100 victories to his credit before taking command of II/JG26 in January '43. Here he talks with the Staffelkapitän of 8/JG26 Oberleutnant Karl Borris (right).

On April 5th, 1943, Geisshardt was shot down by return fire from bombers while on his 642nd sortie. He made a belly landing near Genth, but died in hospital the next day of his injuries.

Oberleutnant Karl Borris in the cockpit of his FW 190 with 20 kill markings painted on its tail.

25

18th March, 1943. 2/JG1 scrambled against a mixed raid of B-17s and B-24s flying at 8,000 metres over Heligoland. In the resulting combat Leutnants Gerhard and Knoke shot down the first Liberators to fall in occupied Europe. Leutnant Gerhard made his attack on the formation leader of the 93rd Bomb Group and waded into the midst of the formation to shoot the bomber out of formation. Return fire was intense and Gerhard's Me 109 was hit. With his aircraft in flames Gerhard baled out, but was found to be dead when he landed. This photograph was taken immediately before the flight.

And so the story is told back at Jever. From left to right: Leutnant Heinz Knoke, Leutnant Schmude (injured) and Hauptmann Hugo Frey.

In early April '43 JG11 was formed from parts of JG1. The first Kommodore was 30 year old Ritterkreuz holder, Major Anton Mader. II/JG11 (formed from I/JG1) remained at Jever under the command of Hauptmann Beise. Here the 5th Staffel are at readiness.

It was proposed that it would be possible to literally bomb the bomber formations. To that end the experimental unit Erprobungskommando 25 carried out tests with 250 Kg bombs. At Jever 2/JG1 (later 5/JG11) also carried out tests. Here a 250 Kg bomb is fitted to an Me 109G.

27

On 23rd March, 1943, Leutnant Knoke reported dropping a bomb on the wing of a B-17. The bomber, he said, fell straight into the sea 30 Km west of Heligoland. The US 8th Air Force did not send any bomber formations out this day.

This reported success prompted a flurry of excitement within the RLM Reichsluftfaht-ministerium. Oberst Lützow visited Jever to find out for himself. The photo shows Lützow with the 6th Staffel Kapitän Hauptmann Falkensamer.

Oberst Günther Lützow was by this time holder of the Ritterkreuz with Oak Leaves and Swords. He was respected by fighter pilots of all ranks and came into conflict with Göring for supporting his men.

A particularly appropriate badge was devised for JG11 in March '43 and adopted as the official badge in April. Oberst Lützow tries out a machine of the new 6th Staffel already emblazoned with the badge. Although holding several staff posts Lützow continued to fly operationally.

FW 190 pilots of III/JG26 waste no time in raising their undercarriages on this scramble.

The sortie over, a pilot receives congratulations from a comrade. Another victory perhaps?

And more hand shaking back in England. 'Knock-out Dropper', 41-24605 of the 303rd Bomb Group, had taken part in 49 missions by November '43, more raids than any other bomber. The plane went on to complete 75 missions before being retired and returned to America. Here pilot 1/Lt. Malcolm E. Brown (without hat) shakes hands with second pilot Captain George T. Mackin. Incredibly not one crew man was ever injured while flying in 'Knock-out Dropper'.

8/JG26 at Wewelghem in Belgium.

Leutnant Karl Borris rose to command I/JG26 and survived the war as a Major with 43 victories, including 4 four engined bombers. He received his Ritterkreuz in November '44.

Leutnant Eder and Unteroffizier Koall of 12/JG2 at Beaumont le Roger. 22 year old Georg-Peter Eder was shot down 17 times and wounded 12 times, but survived the war.

Professor Willy Messerschmitt and his chief test pilot Flugkapitän Fritz Wendel.

The Me 262 was the world's first fully operational jet fighter. In June, 1939, Professor Willy Messerschmitt proposed to the *Reichsluftfahrtministerium* (Reich Air Ministry) in Berlin a fighter far ahead of its time, with a top speed of 900 Km/hr. The project was given the designation P-1065, and was to be powered by two jet engines, the development of which was entrusted to both BMW and Jumo, both leading aero engine manufacturers.

The first prototype, the Me 262 V-1, was powered by a Jumo 210 piston engine in the nose as no jet engine was ready for flight tests. A year later the first jet engines, BMW 003s, were ready for installation and took to the air on March 25th, 1942. The Jumo 210 was retained as a precaution against jet engine failure, which was just as well. On the maiden flight both jets failed just after take off at 50 metres, but test pilot Fritz Wendel landed safely.

On July 18th, 1942, the Me 262 V-3, equipped with Jumo 004 engines, was ready for testing at Leipheim, near Ulm. The new engine was a breakthrough and, by early '43, some leading fighter pilots were given the opportunity to fly the jet. General der Jagflieger Galland and Göring came to see this new wonder plane in July and went away firmly convinced that this was exactly what the Luftwaffe needed.

In November, 1943, Galland and his staff were devastated by Hitler's dictate that the Me 262 must be adapted as a fast bomber 'before' becoming operational as a fighter. This decision proved disastrous for the Luftwaffe for it was a full year before the fighters could go into combat, another chance had been thrown away.

Leipheim airfield, near Ulm. The Me 262 V-3 is prepared for its maiden flight on July 19th, 1942.

Fritz Wendel leaves the cockpit of the V-3. Wire grills have been fitted to the intakes as it was feared that birds would be ingested into the engines.

In February, 1943, JG26 replaced JG54 on the Russian Front. I/JG26, under the command of Johannes Seifert, went to Rjelbitzi, then to Dno, Schatalowka, Ossinowka and Orel. In May Seifert went on a fighter leaders' course and was replaced by Major Losigkeit. In June '43 the Geschwader returned to France and in November Seifert returned as Kommandeur II/JG26. Major Losigkeit (left) and Major Seifert pose for the camera.

After their move from Russia, III/JG54 under 34 year old Major Reinhard Seiler, the most successful pilot of Spanish Civil War, took up residence at Vendeville, near Lille. Although an independent unit, III/JG54 came under the operational control of JG26 for operational purposes. On the left is Heinz Schumann (15/JG2), Major Priller (back to camera) and on the right is Reinhard Seiler.

Pilots of 9/JG54 under Ritterkreuz holder Hauptmann Hans-Ekkehard Bob (centre) prepare for an operation. On the right of Bob is another Ritterkreuz holder, Oberfeldwebel Eugen-Ludwig Zweigart. He was shot down over the Normandy beaches on June 8th, 1944 with a total of 69 victories to his credit.

May 14th, 1943, General Galland visits II/JG11 at Jever. Here Hauptmann Günter Specht shows him the finer points of his 109G.

Major Adolf Dickfeld led II/JG11 for a short time at the beginning of May '43. Later that month Hauptmann Specht took over as Kommandeur of the Gruppe. From the left, Stabsarzt Dr. Perl, Hauptmann Frey, Leutnant Keil, Major Dickfeld and Hauptmann Specht in front of the operations building at Jever.

Most raids took a route over the North Sea to their targets in Germany, this was the area allotted to JG11. Here an Me 109 of 5/JG11 breaks away from a B-17 over Keil during a combat on May 14th, 1943. One of the B-17s engines already in flames. Three B-17s and five B-24s were lost on this raid.

29 year old Hauptmann Wilhelm-Ferdinand Galland, Kommandeur of II/JG26, receives his Ritterkreuz from Major Priller. At the time of the award, 18th May 1943, he had claimed 41 victories.

Oberleutnant Kurt Ebersberger (left), Staffelkapitän of 4/JG26 and Oberleutnant Hans-George Dipple, 9/JG26, in France.

22nd May, 1943, General Galland makes his first flight in the Me 262. Left to right: Fritz Wendel, Hauptmann Geyer and General der Jagdflieger Galland.

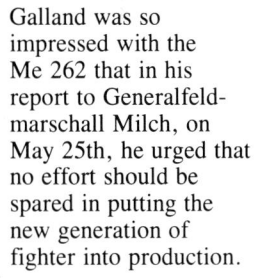

Galland was so impressed with the Me 262 that in his report to Generalfeldmarschall Milch, on May 25th, he urged that no effort should be spared in putting the new generation of fighter into production.

A *Schwarm* (flight of 4) Messerschmitts above the clouds.

'White 5' an Me 109F of III/JG1.

The enemy's view as an Me109G-6 comes in head-on. Two cannon are mounted under the wings.

B-17s of the 390th Bomb Group press on through heavy Flak.

25 year old Oberleutnant Rolf Hermichen began the war flying Me 110s with II/ZG1. In May '42 he joined 3/JG26 as Staffelkapitän and was Kommandeur of the 1st Gruppe JG11 from October '43 to April '44. On one day with JG11 he brought down 4 four engined bombers. By the end of the war he had flown 629 missions and destroyed 64 aircraft, 26 of them heavy bombers. Here Oberleutnant Hermichen (front) is seen with a wounded Allied pilot.

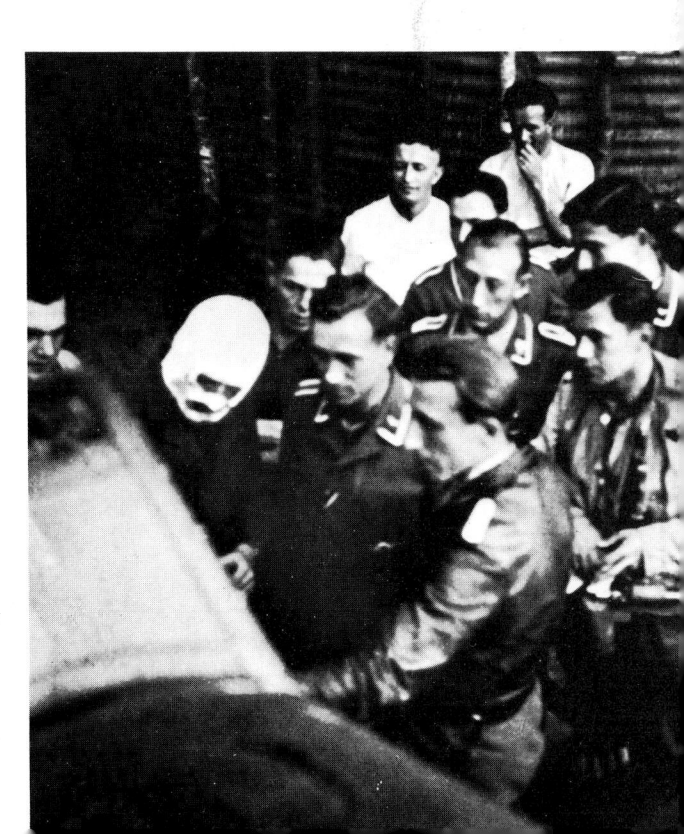

Hauptmann Horst Geyer (second from the left) head of Erprobungskommando 25, meets Generalfeldmarschall Milch and *Rüstungsminister* (Minister of Production) Albert Speer to discuss the weapons under development. Behind Geyer is Oberst Petersen, head of the *Luftwaffen-Erprobungsstellen* (Air Force Test Centres) at Rechlin, Peenemünde and Tarnewitz.

B-24 Liberators were used by RAF Coastal Command on anti U Boat patrols over the Bay of Biscay through which the submarines were bound to travel to reach their French bases on the Atlantic seaboard. As a defence to these patrols the Luftwaffe deployed the Ju 88C-6 equipped *Zerstörer Geschwader* ZG1. In the period of May to September 1943 nine of the Liberators were lost and seven more were damaged by the Ju 88s.

Hauptmann Erwin Clausen, holder of the Ritterkreuz with Oak Leaves, became Kommandeur of I/JG11 at Husum in June '43. By October 10th, 1943, he had shot down a total of 132 aircraft, 14 of which were 4 engined bombers. On this day he failed to return from an attack on American bombers over the North Sea. His place was taken by Hauptmann Hermichen.

June 25th, 1943, the pilots of 5/JG11 celebrated a great day, they had brought down 11 American bombers in a single combat over Keil. These victorious pilots are: Feldwebel Frank carrying the Staffelkapitän, Leutnant Heinz Knoke, on his shoulders; left, Gefreiter Schwertfeger and right Feldwebel Zink.

The 5th Staffel take a 30 minute break at Jever. Although the engagement reportedly took place over Keil, the 8th Air Force target was Wangerooge Island, about 75 miles to the west. 15 B-17s of the 1st Bomb Wing were lost.

More of the victorious '5th' as they swop tales of the great day. Here they have only just landed and are still in their life jackets, the expressions on their faces a reflection of the hard fought battle. Left to right: Fw. Lennartz, Fw. Fest, Uffz Bartelmess, Lt. Trockels and Lt. Knoke. In the combat Fw. Fest destroyed a B-17 with a 250 Kg bomb.

41

In spite of the heavy damage inflicted by fighters and flak many crews brought their bombers back home again. Top, l/Lt. Paul and his crew pose by the shattered ball turrent of their 91st Bomb Group B-17 'Little Miss Mischief' which was hit by flak on October 10th, 1944. The ball gunner, Sergeant Ed Abdo was lucky to escape with his life. Below, Another 91st BG. B-17 42-5225 'Stormy Weather' after over running Bassingbourn's runway on returning from the Ruhr on March 4th, 1943. It was repaired but was lost on operations five months later, on August 17th, 1943.

A wounded gunner is taken away on a stretcher at Kimbolton, home of the 379th Bomb Group.

Erprobungskommando 25 (later Jagdgruppe 10)

Erprobungskommando 25 was established under the command of Oberst Petersen at Wittmundhafen in 1942, and moved to Achmer the following year. The specific task of the unit was the development, testing and introduction into service of specialised air-to-air weapons for use against the four engined bombers.

Five main types of aircraft were tested at Achmer, fitted with various weapons, which were the Me 109, FW 190, Me 110, Me 210 and Me 410. In the last days of the war the following projects were reported as being still under development.

1. 21 cm smoke grenade for fitting to Me 109, FW 190, Me 110 and Me 410.
2. RZ65 Rockets.
3. R4M Rockets.
4. MK108 mounted vertically.
5. Weapons fired automatically by sensors.
6. 400 metre long cables to be towed with explosives attached.
7. Remotely controlled Henschel Hs 293 flying bomb.
8. Fritz X 1800 kg guided bomb.
9. Spraying of chemicals to render perspex canopies opaque.
10. Vertical installation of 33, 21 cm smoke grenades in an He 177.

By the end of July '44 Hauptmann Horst Geyer established a second specialist unit on similar lines to introduce the Me 262 into service, this became Erprobungskommando Me 262. Erpr. Kdo. 25 then moved to Parchim, and finally Redlin. Major Georg Christl took over the command in late '44 and the unit was renamed Jagdgruppe 10.

In September, 1943, General der Jagdflieger Adolf Galland made the journey to Achmer to visit Erprobungskommando 25. L–R: Galland, Geyer, Kornatzki, Trautloft, Lützow, Hardke, Neumann. Note the BK5 50 mm cannon fitted experimentally to these Me 410A-1/U4s.

Hauptmann Horst Geyer, to the right of Galland, explains the workings and tactics of the 21 cm mortars mounted under the wings of this Me 109.

On the wing of one of the 410s. These aircraft were to be used for development of the BK5 and did not carry the standard forward firing armament. L–R: Galland, Oberst Lützow, Hauptmann Geyer and Oberleutnant Hardke. Note the telescopic ZFR 4a gun sight for the BK5 cannon.

The BK5 cannon had a 21 round magazine fitted into the fuselage. Trials of the *Pulk Zerstörer* formation destroyer, Me 410s proved successful and II/ZG26 was re-formed to be equipped with an improved Me 410 retaining its two MG151 cannon and two MG17s in the nose.
The aim of both the BK5 and 21 cm mortar was to break up large formations while staying out of range of the bombers' return fire.

Oberleutnant Hardke explains the principle of the explosive charge and cable device to Oberst Hannes Trautloft and Oberstleutnant Eduard Neumann from the staff of the General der Jagdflieger.

The weapons of war look deceptively harmless when displayed on a table, yet these could break up a heavy bomber formation and allow fighters to pick off any bomber which may be unfortunate enough to drop out of formation without exposing the fighters themselves to the murderous cross fire from the bomber boxes.

Major Sherman R. Beaty, Commander of the 555th Squadron, 386th Bombardment Group (Medium). The 386th was one of the B-26 Marauder equipped units in the 8th Air Force which undertook many of the early raids on France in August and September '43. In October the unit was transferred to the 9th Air Force which was to specialise in tactical bombing as oppposed to the 8th's rôle of strategic bombing.

One of the first B-17 crews to operate from English bases pose for the camera man.

Amongst the early targets for the 8th Air Force were the Luftwaffe, airfields in occupied France. This is Amiens/Glisy under attack.

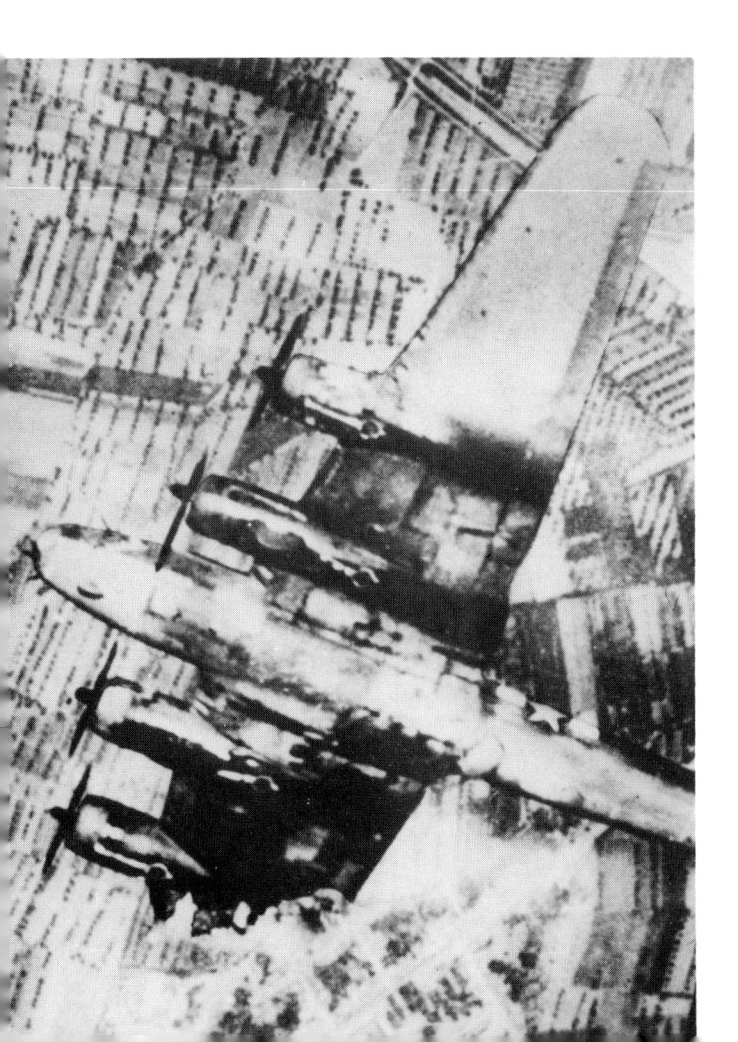

The 97th and 301st Bomb Groups transferred from the 8th to the 12th Air Force in North Africa in November '42. This B-17 received a direct hit from Flak and went down near Naples. Five men got out.

Others were luckier. This is 42-31471 of the 303rd Bomb Group which was hit by a 20 mm cannon shell. The aircraft was lost later, on March 8th, 1944.

In the Summer of '43 II/JG26 carried out the first operation with the 21 cm Mortars. It soon became clear, however, that the addition of this equipment to a single engined fighter reduced its performance to an unacceptable level, endangering both machine and pilot. For this reason the mortars were passed on to the *Zerstörer* units equipped with Me 110s and Me 410s.

The battle hardened face of a fighter pilot; 22 year old Feldwebel Wilhelm Hofmann of JG26 in 1943. Despite the loss of his left eye he remained with his unit where his determination against the heavy bombers resulted in the destruction of seven. He was awarded the Ritterkreuz in October '44 and was killed on March 26th, 1945 after a total of 44 victories, all scored on the West Front.

31 year old Leutnant Kurt Goltzsch, Kapitän 5/JG2 (left of group) after bringing down this Spitfire over France. He had joined JG2 as an Unteroffizier and scored 14 victories in Tunisia. II/JG2 were based at Vitry en Artois in the summer of '43. On September 4th, 1943, he seriously injured his back after being shot down by Spitfires over the Channel and suffered partial paralysis. By this time he had 43 victories and was awarded the Ritterkreuz in February '44. He never recovered from his injuries and died in hospital on September 26th, 1944.
Below. Hauptmann Kurt Bühligen presents Goltzsch with his Deutsche Kreuz in Gold.

On November 13th, 1943, 'Sepp' Wurmheller was awarded the Oak Leaves to his Ritterkreuz in recognition of his success on the Channel Front after claiming 60 victories. This photo shows Wurmheller when Kapitän of 9/JG2.

Professor Kurt Tank (left) with his project engineer, Ludwig Mittelhuber, in Bad Eilsen.

The RAF's heavy night attacks began in earnest in May and June, 1942, with attacks on Cologne, Essen and Bremen. The RLM issued a specification for a new night fighter design. Heinkel, Focke-Wulf and Junkers expressed an interest and submitted designs. Dipl. Ing. Kurt Tank proposed a twin engined night fighter, the main structure of which was to be made from wood, along similar lines to the Mosquito, examples of which had now been captured.

Nine months later, on July 1st, 1943, Focke-Wulf test pilot Hans Sanders took off from Hanover-Langenhagen in the Ta 154 V-1 (TE+FE) for the first flight. In recognition of his work Kurt Tank had been made a Professor in January '43 and was allowed to prefix his design after his name, hence Ta 154.

The Ta 154 V-1 was powered by two Jumo 211F/N engines and was capable of 635 Km/hr at 6,000 metres. Soon the aircraft became known as the *Hölzernen Wunder*, imitating the Mosquito again.

The factory which produced the glue used to hold the wings of the aircraft together was destroyed shortly after production began and alternative glues were not up to the job. Several pre-production aircraft crashed in tests when their wings fell apart in the air. Kurt Tank stopped production of wings, but was then accused of sabotaging the programme by Göring. The Ta 154 never went into full scale production, but there was a proposal to use some finished airframes as flying bombs from which the pilot could escape before the Ta 154 exploded amidst a bomber formation. None of these were even flown.

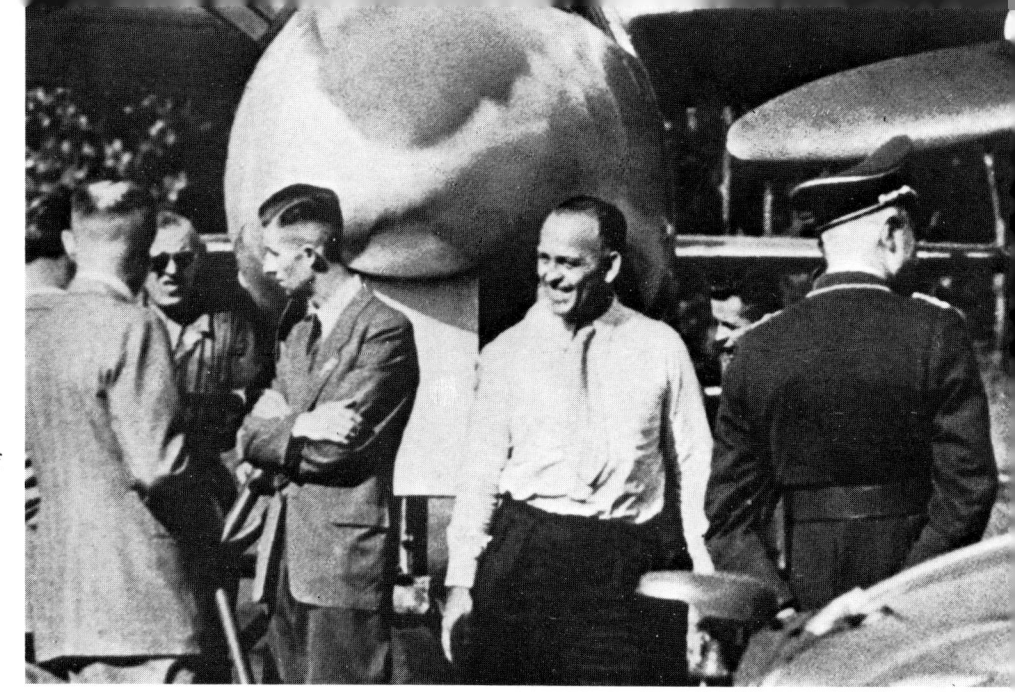

Professor Tank (in shirt) and some of the development team in front of the Ta 154-V1 at Hannover-Langenhagen.

Not only was Tank the designer of the Ta 154, but he also acted as one of the test pilots. Kurt Tank, it seemed, had an affinity with his creations. The first flight of the Ta 154 V-1 was made by Flugkapitän Hans Sander on July 1st, 1943.

The 'Wooden Wonder' TE+FE is guided into the disperal after Kurt Tank's flight. Satisfied with his creation Tank climbs out. The Ta 154 was never made operational, although production lines were set up.

The gaily emblazoned nose of Kurt Tank's most famous creation, the FW 190. Under the cowling is the powerful BMW 801D fourteen cylinder radial air cooled engine which gave the fighter its formidable performance.
The *Tatzelwurm* again appears on this machine which is from the 5th Staffel JG1.

On July 1st, 1943, Major Egon Mayer took over command of JG2. Two weeks later, at 07.40 hrs, July 14th, he brought down this B-17 of the 331st Squadron, 94th Bomb Group, near Anthony-sur-Seine. Captain Kee H. Harrison landed the stricken bomber, with a full bomb load, in a cornfield. The crew escaped but were captured and sat out the war in Stalag. XVII B. Here Major Mayer examines his prize which was repaired and later flew with KG200.

B-17F 41-24585 'Wulfe-Hound' became the first Fortress to be flown by the Luftwaffe. 'Wulfe-Hound' was brought down in France on December 12th, 1942, when being flown by Lt. Paul F. Flickinger of the 303rd Bomb Group on a mission to Rouen. After examination at Rechlin, the B-17 went on a week long tour of fighter stations, this stop being Poix.

The end of a P-38 Lightning. Its distinctive shape became a common sight in the skies over Europe, but it was superseded as a bomber escort by the P-47 and P-51 later in the war.

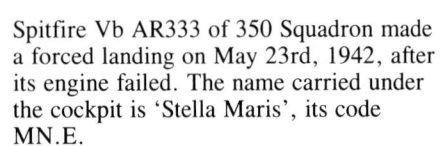

Spitfire Vb AR333 of 350 Squadron made a forced landing on May 23rd, 1942, after its engine failed. The name carried under the cockpit is 'Stella Maris', its code MN.E.

Feldwebel Wenneckers (above) and Unteroffizier Lennartz (right) two of the most successful pilots with 5/JG11 at Jever. Both these pilots flew the majority of their missions against the bomber formations and were among the few who survived the war.

Helmut Lennartz very nearly didn't survive. This is what was left of his Me 109 after a collision on landing at dusk. The second aircraft was being towed across the airfield by a mechanic, a practice which was against regulations. Both men were lucky to get away with no more than a bad fright.

During 1943 small fighter units were formed at aircraft production plants throughout Germany. Their primary purpose was to protect the aircraft factories from attack and were known as *Industriestaffeln*. In August, 1943, Jagdgruppe 50 was formed at Wiesbaden-Erbenheim, to support these Staffeln. Commander of Jagdgruppe 50 was major Hermann Graf (seen here left) with another Ritterkreuz holder, Oberfeldwebel Ernst Süss, at Wiesbaden-Erbenheim.

Industriestaffeln were formed at Tutow, Hannover-Langenhagen, Oschersleben, Kassel-Waldau, Augsburg, Leipzig-Mockau, Weiner-Neustadt and Regensburg. They were equipped with either Me 109s or FW 190s depending upon which was produced locally. These are factory fresh Me 109G-6/R6s, this being the variant fitted with the underwing MG151 cannon.

Major Hermann Graf and Major Herbert Ihlefeld attend a meeting at Bad Aibling. Major Ihlefeld was Kommandeur of Jagdgruppe 25 which was formed at Staken in June '43 and operated from Gadelegen in August '43. The Gruppe flew high altitude variants of the 109 to intercept reconnaissance Mosquitos.

In early 1943, I/JG4 was established in Rumania to protect the vital oil installations from attacks launched from North Africa. They had not long to wait, for on August 1st 'Operation Tidalwave' was launched.

Two groups of B-24 Liberators from the 9th and three groups from the 8th Air Force took 179 bombers to the oil plant at Ploesti. The target was left in flames, but the cost was high, 53 B-24s and 532 air crew did not return.

Rosarius's Amazing Circus

The second Staffel of Versuchsverband Ob.d.L acquired the name Rosarius's Circus after its commander Hauptmann Rosarius. The purpose of the circus was to tour operational Luftwaffe units to demonstrate the performance of enemy aircraft that pilots could expect to meet in combat. This also gave them an opportunity to examine their enemy at close quarters and discover any weakenesses a particular aircraft may have.

The aircraft used had all been captured after landing in Europe and had their markings changed to prominently display the German markings. Although the upper surface colours were usually retained, the undersides and tail units were painted bright yellow, another precaution to guard against their misidentification. The aircraft were also kept fully armed with live ammunition, but they were never intended to be used in action.

A look into the cockpit of a Spitfire IX, T9+EK. 2/Versuchsverband Ob.d.L. operated three Spitfires.

The giant P-47 Thunderbolt, T9+FK. To keep as close as possible to the original colours the captured aircraft kept the original upper surface colours, but the tail and undersides were re-painted in yellow.

The North American P-51 Mustang, believed by many to be the finest escort fighter, had the range to escort bombers right into the heart of Germany. Note the small code 'T9' of Versuchsverband Ob.d.L, the 'Circus' was officially the 2nd Staffel. This was one of two captured Mustangs to crash during the first half of 1944. Not being familiar with the charactistics of its laminar flow wings the pilots got into incipient spins with insufficient height to recover.

Oberstleutnant Helmut Lent tries the cockpit of T9+FK for size. Lent was a legend among night fighter pilots, holder of the Ritterkreuz with Oak Leaves, Swords and Diamonds with 102 victories, all but 8 scored at night.

A pilot is briefed on T9+FK while others watch Rosarius's Circus performing.

59

'Wulfe-Hound' during her tour of fighter stations. Here she is at Jever to allow the pilots and ground crew of II/JG11 to inspect the *Fliegende Festung* at close quarters. The white outlined panels on engine cowlings and wings indicate the particularly vulnerable areas for the benefit of the pilots.

Twenty-nine year old Hauptmann Günther Specht began his career flying Me 110s with I/ZG26, but lost his left eye when he was shot down over the North Sea on December 3rd, 1939. After a series of staff posts he became Kommandeur of II/JG11 in May '43. His slight build led to his being named 'Little Specht'.

This Stirling was brought down by pilots of II/JG11 flying at night from Wittmundhafen during the summer of 1943.

Many of the victories over the *Viermot* literally 'four motors', as the heavy bombers were known, were gained by pilots flying the Me 109G-6. The G-6 carried a basic armament of a 30 mm cannon firing through the nose and two MG 131 13 mm machine guns above the engine. Two 'Rüstsatz' versions were available to add weapons beneath the wings; the R-4 with two 30 mm MK 108s and R-6 with two MG 151 20 mm cannon.

General der Jagdflieger Adolf Galland lost both of his younger brothers in fighter combat. 29 year old Major Wilhelm-Ferdinand Galland flew with II/JG26 on the Channel Front, became Staffelkapitän of 5/JG26 in May '42 and Kommandeur of II Gruppe in January '43.

Major Egon Mayer, who became Kommodore of JG2 on July 1st, 1943, pays his respects to a fallen comrade.

Wilhelm Galland received the Ritterkreuz in May '43, but was shot down on August 17th, 1943, by Thunderbolts during an attack on American bombers in the Leige area. At the time of his death, Wilhelm had brought down 55 aircraft, 8 of them four engined bombers.

The youngest Galland brother was Paul. He flew with 8/JG26 and was a Leutnant with 17 victories when he was shot down by Spitfires and killed on October 31st, 1942. Here Paul (right) inspects a captured troop carrier with Major Priller, his Gruppen Kommandeur.

Oberleutnant Hans Ehlers in the FW 190 of the Geschwader Adjutant. Ehlers became Staffelkapitän of 3/JG1 on November 1st, 1943, and Kommandeur of I Gruppe in May '44. At the time of his death over the Eifel mountains on December 27th, 1944, he had destroyed at least 54 aircraft, including 20 heavy bombers. He had been awarded the Ritterkreuz that July and had been nominated for the Oak Leaves.

A daunting sight to the Luftwaffe fighter pilots, be they novice or *Experten*. A formation of B-17s in tight formation.
A total of 76 B-17 crews took refuge in neutral Switzerland during the war.

2/Lt. Stephen P. Rapport's crew was among them. Unable to make the return flight from their third mission — Regensburg, on August 17th, 1943 — Rapport elected to land at Utzensdorf, near Bern. The aircraft is 42-30315 'Peg of my Heart' from the 390th Bomb Group.

Kommandeur II/JG26, Major Johannes Seifert returns from a sortie over the Channel on September 9th, 1943. By this time he had brought down a considerable number of aircraft, including eleven over Russia with I/JG26 between February and May, 1943.

'Pips' Priller Kommodore JG26 from January 11th, 1943, to January 27th, 1945. In the summer of '43 he was promoted to Oberstleutnant. Of his twenty victories during his time as Kommodore, nine were four engined bombers.

Streaking vapour trails behind them another bomber formation makes its way to Germany.

In the autumn of '43 Hauptmann Anton Hackl took over command of III/JG11. 28 year old 'Toni' Hackl, was awarded the Ritterkreuz on May 27th, 1942, after 48 victories and the Oak Leaves less than three months later, on August 6th, after bringing his score to 104 aircraft destroyed.

24 year old Oberleutnant Gerhard Sommer, Staffelkapitän of 4/JG11, after bringing down another *Viermot*. Of his 20 victories, 14 were heavy bombers. He was awarded the Ritterkreuz posthumously after being shot down over Lippstadt, Westphalia, on May 12th, 1944. In the picture above Major Specht Kommandeur II/JG11 is wearing the sun glasses and right is Kommodore, Oberstleutnant Mader.

Major Kurt Bühligen, Kommandeur II/JG2, in the operations room at Criel.

Major Bühligen and Leutnant Müngerstorf, Adjutant of the Gruppenstab II/JG2 at Cambrai-Epinoy.

Bühligen (right) greets the Messerschmitt Chief Test Pilot, Flugkapitän Fritz Wendel, arriving at Epinoy in an Me 109G.

Oberleutnant Johannes Naumann served with JG26 from the outbreak of war. He was awarded the Ritterkreuz in November '44 and joined JG7 flying Me 262s in April '45. He had 34 victories, all on the West Front, 7 of which were heavy bombers.

Some Me 109s of IV/JG3 'Udet' were fitted with the 21 cm rockets and used against the 15th Air Force on the Italian Front from July to September, 1943.

26 year old Hans 'Fips' Phillip was the second Luftwaffe pilot to surpass the 200 victory mark. On April 1st, 1943, he became Kommodore of JG1 but was shot down on October 8th over Nordhorn by P-47s. In his six months in the West he brought down 29 aircraft, only one of which was a four engined bomber.

Hauptmann Kurt Ebersberger, Staffelkapitän of 4/JG26, was shot down and killed on October 24th, 1943. He had brought down a total of 27 aircraft.

The sort of damage that 20 mm cannon can inflict upon a Fortress. This is B-17 42-3190, Major Egon Mayer's victim of July 14th, 1943.

I/JG27 moved from their bases in France to the Vienna sector in July '43. Here they operated until the invasion of Europe forced a return to France. This is the 3rd Staffel in October '43 at Fels am Agram.

I/JG27 scramble.

Adolf Galland paid I/JG27 a visit in October. Left to right are Galland, Oberst Handrick and Oberstleutnant Neumann.

On October 19th, 1943, Hermann Göring visited pilots at Wiesbaden-Erbenheim. Before the Reichmarschall's inspection Oberst Lützow and General Galland exchange a few words with the men. Left is Oberst Günther von Malzahn.

Pleasant enough here, but the Reichmarschall was not always so affable towards his men. He often flew into a rage, accusing his commanders of letting him, and the Fatherland, down.

The ball bearing manufacturing centre of Schweinfurt became one of the costliest single targets attacked by the US 8th Air Force. The first raid of 230 B-17s was launched on August 17th, 1943, — 36 bombers were lost. On October 14th, the mission was repeated, this time 60 of the 290 B-17s were lost to Flak, day and night fighters. This is the crew of Bud J. Peaslee, Task Force Commander for the second Schweinfurt raid.

Fortresses of the 390th Bomb Group were luckier than most, losing only one of fifteen crews sent to the ball bearing plant.

October '43. An Me 109G-6 in front of the No. 1 hangar at Jever. The two pilots, Fuhrmann and Trockels of 5/JG11, lost their lives in the defence of their country.

Hauptmann Falkenshamer, Kapitän 6/JG11, and Hauptmann Specht celebrate in front of the operations building at Jever. On Christmas Day, 1943, Falkensamer took off and did not come back.

General Oberst Stumpff visited the FW 190 equipped I/JG11 at Husum in November '43. The Kapitän of 3 Staffel, 22 year old Oberleutnant Hans-Heinrich König, salutes the General. König lost an eye when flying a night fighter with III/NJG3, but went on to become a successful FW 190 pilot.

On November 17th, 1943, Göring called the pilots of the three Jagdgeschwadern then charged with the defence of the Reich to a meeting at Achmer.

Here he turned on his faithful men, saying that it was they who were responsible for the 'unsatisfactory results' and letting the bombers through.

After the rebuke a fatherly gesture towards Major von Kornatzki, Kommandeur of the Sturmgruppe JG4.

Oberstleutnant Hermann Graf, who came from the Russian Front and JG50 to command JG11. He was only the fifth pilot to receive the Diamonds to his Ritterkreuz.

General Diesing (left) describes a modern fighter pilot's equipment to the Reichmarschall. Left to right: Diesing, Hauptmann von Brauchitsch, Major Christl, Hauptmann Thierfelder, Hauptmann Geyer, Göring, Oberstleutnant Herrmann and Oberst Trautloft.

November 25th, 1943, was a black day for JG26. Oberstleutnant Johannes Seifert, the long serving Gruppenkommandeur, took off with the 6th and 8th Staffeln to intercept a force of 30 P-38 Lightnings over Bethune, France. 'Hannes' dived into the P-38s, but misjudged his attack and clipped the right wing of one. Both aircraft went down, the Lightning spinning with flames enveloping its port wing and engine, to crash near Lacouture.
Siefert had flown 439 sorties and brought down 54 aircraft, including two Fortresses.
Above; Oberstleutnant Priller, Geschwaderkommodore JG26 pays his last respects to Seifert and another three of his pilots.

JG53 'Pik As' – Ace of Spades Geschwader operated on the Mediterranean Front, Tunisia, Sicily, southern and northern Italy from 1943 to the end of the war.

Hauptmann Jürgen Harder received his Ritterkreuz in December '43. In 1944 he became Kommandeur I/JG53, and Kommodore JG11 in January '45. The Harder family lost three sons in the war, all were fighter pilots. Jürgen died on February 17th, 1945, when he crashed at Straussberg near Berlin. 9 of his 64 victories were heavy bombers. Behind is Franz Götz.

Hauptmann Götz served throughout the war and was Kommandeur III/JG53. He went on to command JG26 and ended the war with 63 victories.
Above; an Me 109G-6 of JG53 has its weaponry harmonized.

In the hard fought years of '43 and '44, 31 year old Leo Schuhmacher flew with II/JG1 and ended the war flying with the Me 262 equipped JV44. He received the Ritterkreuz on March 1st, 1945, and shot down 23 aircraft, including 10 four engined bombers.

27 year old Herbert Rollwage flew with II/JG53 in Russia and the Mediterranean before joining the *Reichsverteidigung* units at the end of '43. He shot down more four engined bombers than any other pilot, an incredible 44 by the end of the war. He received his Ritterkreuz on April 6th, 1944, and the Oak Leaves on January 21st, 1945. His total victories amounted to 102.

Another B-17 comes to grief. This is B-17F 42-97474 of the 381st Bomb Group which was brought down on February 22nd, 1944, whilst being flown by 1/Lt. Francis N. Fridgen. The 381st lost six B-17s on this raid.

77

The FW 190A-6 of 3/JG1's Staffelkapitän Oberleutnant Hans Ehlers receives some attention.

'Black 3' an FW 190 of I/JG1 takes off across the snow. Under the fuselage is a jettisonable 300 Litre fuel tank.

Taking up position for the coup de grâce, this B-17 is already done for. The left engine is in flames and the undercarriage hangs limply down. The tail and starboard elevator hang in tatters. It must be concluded that the rear gunner is either dead or unable to return fire as the fighter pilot would not have put himself in this suicidal position otherwise.

Liberators trailing their long banners of contrails behind them make for Germany.

One of the first Mustangs to escort bombers over Germany, this is a P-51 B, easily distinguished from the later P-51 D which had a bubble canopy. Here the underwing tanks are being fitted, one of the secrets of the type's great endurance.

Me 109Gs of JG27 flying from the Vienna area. The Geschwaderstab, I, II, and III Gruppen were all based here until the invasion of Europe forced a move to France.

General der Jagdflieger Galland at a meeting held in the beginning of '44 to discuss the defence of the oil fields in Rumania. The photo was taken at Mizil in Rumania. Left to right: Major Kurt Ubben (Kommandeur III/JG77), Galland, Oberst Woldenga (Fliegerführer Balkan) and Oberstleutnant Neumann (Jafü Rumänien).

Heavy explosions, the work of the Me 110 units, such as these were intended to un-nerve the bomber crews and split up the close formations.

As yet the heavy bombers were still without fighter escort at their extreme range. On January 13th, 1944, 4/ZG76 took off from Neubiberg, near Munich, where they engaged P-38 Ligntnings with their BK5 50 mm cannon.

The P-38 Lightning was, at this time, still the mainstay of the escort fighters when equipped with long range tanks.

With the continuing onslaught of RAF night bombing, desperate measures were needed to increase the night fighter force. Major Hajo Herrmann suggested that pilots experienced in night flying should roam freely in the bomber streams. This became known as *Wilde Sau* 'Wild Boar', as opposed to the traditional ground controlled night fighting system 'Tame Boar'. JG300 was the first such unit to form, using mainly old JG11 aircraft.

Here a meeting is held at Deelen, home of the night fighter unit NJG3. Left: Major Graf (JG11), 3rd Left: Hptm. Specht (II/JG11) 4th Left: Major Lent (NJG3).

III/JG300 were formed at Oldenburg and took over the aircraft of III/JG11.

A most unusual way to leave your aircraft! This feat was accomplished at Gabbert, a satellite of Märkisch/Friedland. The aircraft is an Me 109G-6 of EJG1.

Oberst Walter Grabmann (centre) Kommandeur of the 3rd Jagddivision, visits I/JG1. Left is Heinz Bär and right Walter Oesau, Kommodore JG1. 38 year old Grabmann had been Kommandeur of the Kondor Legion in Spain.

Major Heinz Bär addresses II/JG1 pilots.

This full size mural of a B-17 was not painted on the hangar doors at Eschborn for fun; its purpose was to help pilots judge their head-on attacks.

Oberstleutnant Egon Mayer, Kommodore JG2, was shot down by Thunderbolts over Montmedy on March 2nd, 1944. He had destroyed a total of 102 aircraft; 25 of them four engined bombers.

March '44 was a bad time for Geschwader Kommodores for on the 20th Oberst Wolf-Deitrich Wilcke of JG3 was shot down by Mustangs near Schöppenstedt. 'Prince' Wilcke was one of the leading lights of the fighter commanders and had brought down 162 aircraft, 25 on the West Front of which 4 were *Viermots*.

32 year old Oberstleutnant Hermann Graf was Kommodore of JG11 from November '43 to April '44. When flying on the Russian Front in 1942 he earned the Ritterkreuz in January, Oak Leaves and Swords in May and Diamonds in September. His daring was legendary; on March 29th, 1944, he shot down two B-17s and was injured when he rammed an escorting fighter. In October he returned to command his old unit, JG52, on the Russian Front and by the end of the war had brought down 212 aircraft. He was captured by American forces and handed to the Russians from whose captivity he was finally released in 1950.

Major Specht was promoted from Kommandeur II/JG11 to Kommodore JG11 in April '44. By this time he had brought down 30 aircraft, as marked on the tail of his aircraft. On April 8th the one eyed *Experten* was awarded the Ritterkreuz. During Operation *Bodenplatte*, on January 1st, 1945, his aircraft was hit by ground fire near Brussels and he was posted missing.

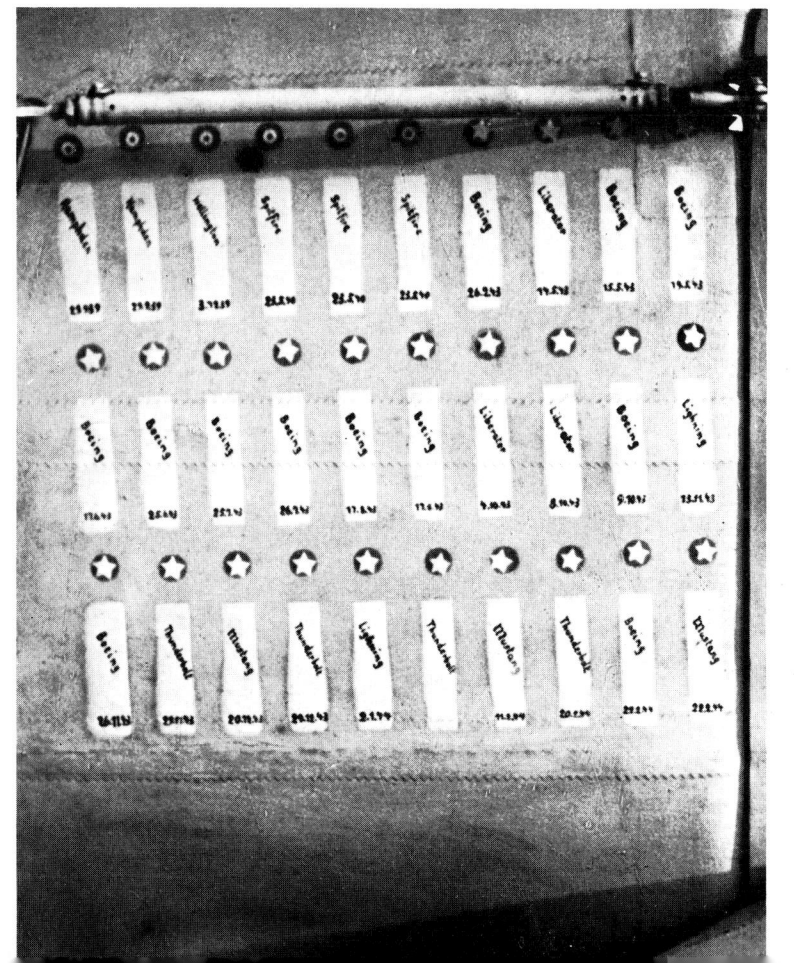

The winter scene at Ansbach, home of 4/ZG76, in March 1944.

In flight over the snow covered French landscape. This Me 110 of ZG76 carries both drop tanks and twin 21 cm rocket tubes.

Oberleutnant Helmut Haugk, one of the most experienced *Zerstörer* pilots, had received his Ritterkreuz when serving with III/ZG26 in the Mediterranean. In October '43 he became Staffelkapitän of 4/ZG76 in defence of the Reich.

On March 16th, 1944, Haugk led twelve Me 110s of his 4th Staffel away from Ansbach on what was to prove their last sortie.

The Me 110s had an escort of Me 109s to protect them as they headed for an incoming bomber formation, but in cloud and bad visability the forces became separated. Now without fighter protection the Me 110s headed straight into a formation of between 150 and 200 bombers, escorted by around 120 Mustangs. Meeting the bombers head-on the 21 cm rockets were fired at a range of 300 metres, then they opened fire with their 20 mm cannon. Several Fortresses were seen to fall before the Mustangs engaged with the Me 110s outnumbered 10:1. Haugk and his wireless operator Hommrichlausen baled out as, one by one, the *Zerstörern* were shot down. Only one aircraft returned to Ansbach, and that was severely damaged.

In pursuit of an Me 110, already the port wing has been hit.

11/JG53 scramble.

8/JG53 on their way to intercept a raid.

The Me 109 of Schwarmführer Leutnant Landt.

A camera gun captures the destruction of a B-17.

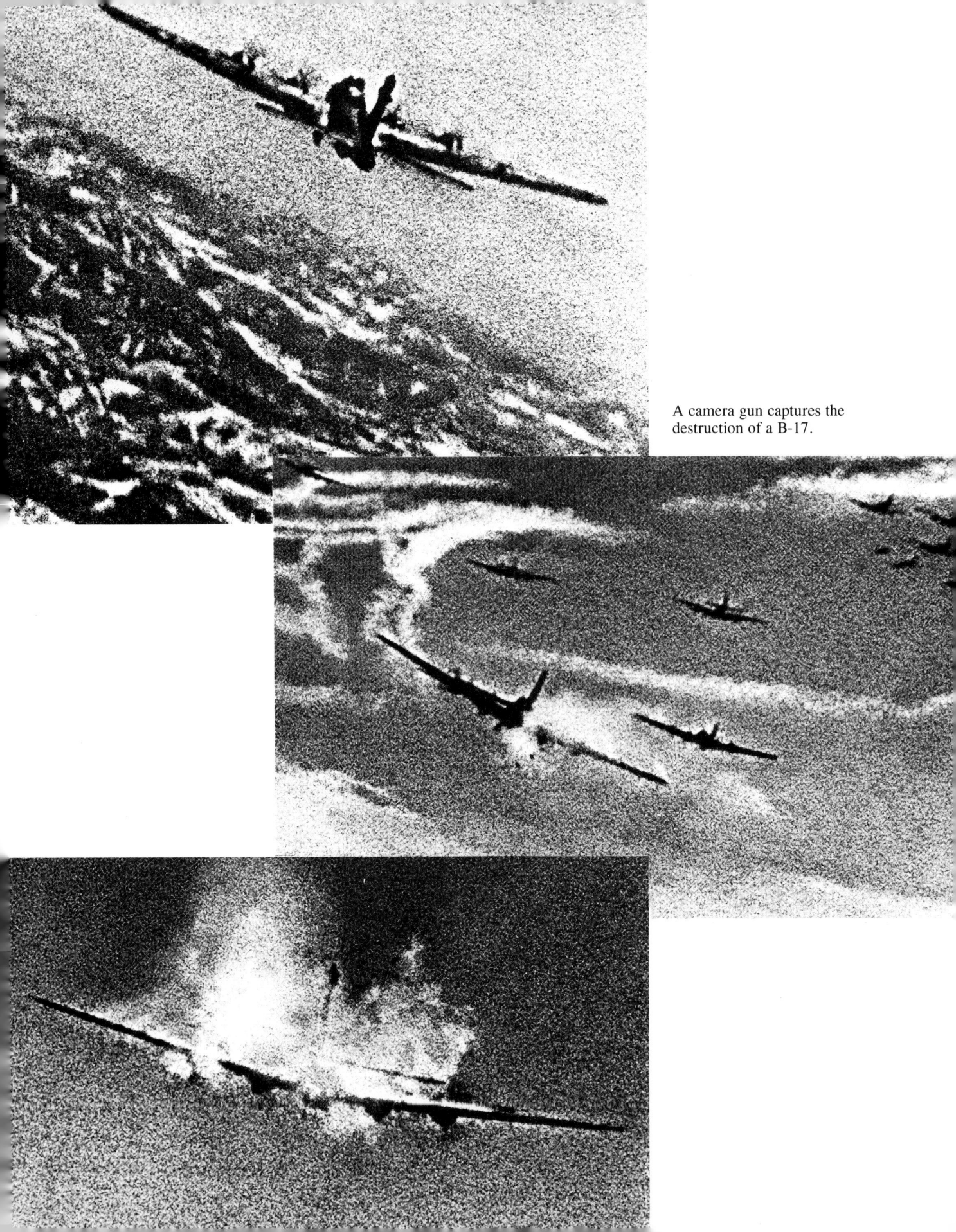

As well as the 8th Air Force operations from England, the 15th Air Force kept defences on the alert on the Mediterranean Front, thus spreading the Luftwaffe's resources still further. The 'Y' on the tails of these machines denotes that they were assigned to the 15th Air Force.

Units flying the heavily armed B-26 Marauder began operations to disrupt communications on April 19th, 1944.

Holder of the Swords to his Ritterkreuz Major Bär, Kommandeur II/JG1, brought down this B-17 near Rheine Airfield on February 22nd, 1944. The Fortress is 42-3040 'Miss Quachita' of Lt. Spencer K. Osterberg from the 91st Bomb Group.

The gunner in a shattered turret like this stood little chance. It was occupied by Sergeant Bostrom. Inspecting the turret are (left to right) Leo Schuhmacher, Bär and Feldwebel Sauer, the long standing Rottenflieger to Oberst Oesau. Two months later, on April 22nd, Bär brought down his 200th aircraft.

Ritterkreuz holder Leutnant Leopold Münster of II/JG3 rammed a bomber over Hildsheim, on May 8th, 1944, but was killed when his aircraft exploded. He had brought down 95 aircraft, 25 of which had been destroyed in the West, and of these at least eight had been *Viermots*.

Dogs made for good mascots, their boisterous welcomes boosting the moral of their owners. This is Leutnant Landt of 8/JG53 with 'Wolf' and his mechanics.

On May 11th, 1944, another Geschwader Kommodore fell in combat. Oberst Walter Oesau, Kommodore JG1 since October '43, was shot down by P-38 Lightnings over the Eifel Mountains. He had brought down 125 aircraft, ten of them heavy bombers.

Walter Oesau found his final resting place at his home town of Meldorf in Holstein. The Kommodore's story ended amidst a sea of flowers.

A true hero's send off as the funeral cortege passes through Meldorf. Below, left to right, General der Jagdflieger Galland, Hauptmann Schmoller-Haldy, Oberst M. Ibel and Major Dahl.

Hauptmann Hans-Heinrich Koenig, Kommandeur I/JG11, was killed on May 24th, 1944. He had become a specialist in the destruction of *Viermots* 19 of his 23 victories being bombers. On this day his 20th bomber exploded under his fire and his FW 190 collided with the wreckage, the port wing was ripped off and the fighter crashed. He was posthumously awarded the Ritterkreuz on the September 2nd.

The high losses suffered by the Luftwaffe fighter arm in 1943 led to the withdrawal of JG300 from *Wilde Sau* night fighter operations to concentrate on day fighter operations. Its sister units, JG301 and JG302, continued to fly night operations for the time being until they too were called upon to join the daylight battles.

Hauptmann Theodor Weissenberger was promoted to Geschwader Kommodore JG7 in January '45. He had 208 victories (33 in the west and 8 flying the Me 262) and held the Ritterkreuz with Oak Leaves. He died in a motor racing accident on the Nurburgring in 1950.

Major Kurt Bühligen, Kommodore JG2, brought down 2 Thunderbolts over the Normandy Beach-head, his 100th and 101st victories. He flew only in the western and southern (Tunisian) theatres and brought down a total of 112 aircraft, 24 of which were heavy bombers.

Galland visited Hauptmann Geyer of Erprobungskommando 25 at Achmer to discuss the weapon developments under his control. On the right of the group is Major Georg Christl, who was on Galland's staff and who soon took over Erpr. Kdo. 25. The aircraft is a Siebel Si 204, often used as a communications machine.

97

On May 10th, 1944, Erprobungsgruppe Me 262 was formed at Lechfeld to make the type operational. 14 pilots under the command of Hauptmann Thierfelder began training on the Me 262 on May 15th.
Here Generalfeldmarschall Milch and Galland, two of the leading advocates of the remarkable jet, make a visit in early July.

Left to right: Erhard Milch, Oberstleutnant Bohland, Galland. Far right: Hauptmann Thierfelder and Oberst Petersen.

The unit became known as Kommando Thierfelder.

Ground crews for the new jets were recruited from III/ZG26. The Stabskompanie at Lechfeld, later 8 Staffel at Leipheim and 9 Staffel at Schwäbisch Hall, worked with Messerschmitt staff to ready the machines for operations.

Some men from the first course at Lechfeld. Left to right: Lt. Schreiber, Ofw. Recker, Jumo engine fitter Peter, unknown, and Fw. Lennartz.

Hauptmann Geyer (right) took over command of the unit on August 5th, 1944, following the death of Thierfelder in a 262 crash. Leutnant 'Bubi' Schreiber made the first Me 262 combat victory claim on July 26th when he destroyed a Mosquito. Centre is Hauptmann Riedel.

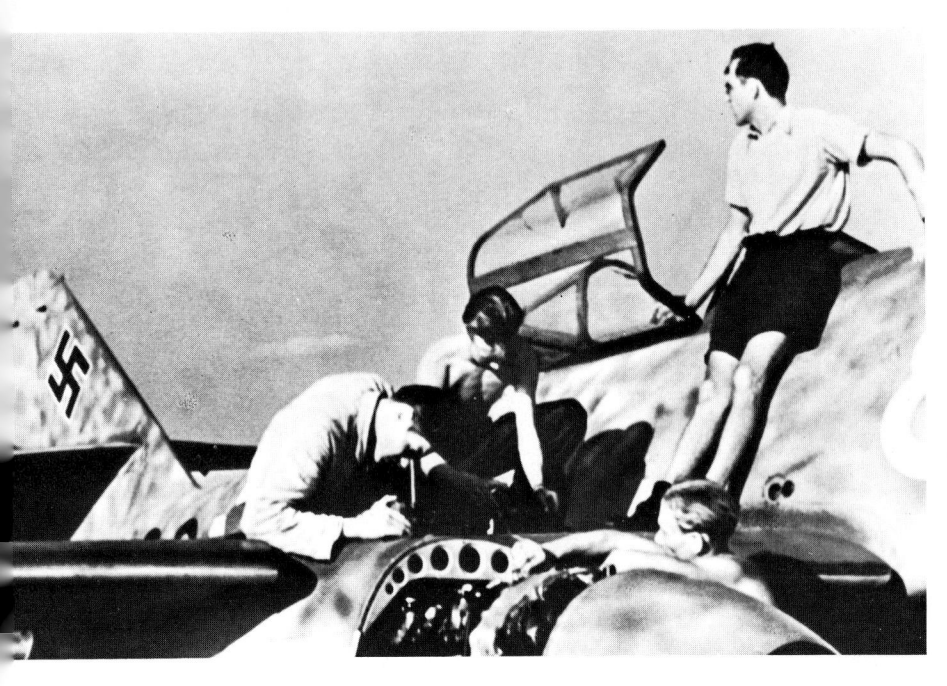

A camera gun was fitted above the starboard engine to assist in verifying claims and to further the tactical development.

It was not long before American fighter pilots began to bring back reports of the new jet and of its phenomenal performance.

26 year old Hauptmann Jürgen Harder had been a successful pilot with JG53 in Russia. He took over as Kommandeur I/JG53 in August '44 and led the unit in the defence of the Rumanian oil fields against the US 15th Air Force.

Josef Wurmheller was promoted from Staffelkapitän 9/JG2 to Major and Kommandeur III/JG2 on June 8th, 1944. Two weeks later, on the 22nd, he collided with his Rottenflieger over the Invasion Beach-head; both men were killed. He had 102 victories, at least 13 *Viermots*, had received the Oak Leaves to his Ritterkreuz and was awarded the Swords posthumously.

Major Klaus Mietusch, Kommandeur III/JG26, awards his pilots with the EK2. On September 17th, 1944, he shot down a Mustang, his 72nd victory, near Aldekirk/Rhineland but was then shot down by another P-51 when landing. He held the Ritterkreuz with Oak Leaves and of his victories 10 were against *Viermots*. He was 26 years old.

Some of the most senior members of the Luftwaffe visited the rocket testing grounds at Peenemünde/West to witness the testing of the Me 163. Centre: Erhard Milch (following Udet's suicide, Generalluftzeugmeister), partly obscured: Albert Speer – Chief of Central Planning Staff, right (in leather coat) Wernher von Braun – head of the rocket establishment Peenemünde/East.

Peenemünde was split into two sections, the establishment in the East section was responsible for the V2 rocket development, while in the West section other developments such as the Me 163 rocket fighter were built. Here the Me 163 V-3 takes off.

Some of the development team of the Me 163: test pilot Hanna Reitsch shakes hands with Professor Messerschmitt whilst in the centre is its designer Dr. Alexander Lippisch.

102

On June 6th, 1944, Allied troops landed in Normandy, the invasion of Fortress Europe had begun. The Luftwaffe, and especially the Reich defence units, now had another front on which to fight. The American 8th and 9th Air Forces as well as the RAF turned away from strategic bombing of Germany to the tactical support of the invasions forces. Only the 15th Air Force, operating from Italy, continued to bomb southern Germany. This afforded a brief respite for the heavily bombed towns of northern Germany which had been robbed of virtually all their fighter defences.

At one stage only I/JG300, equipped with high altitude Me 109s, was left and the future of the two *Wilde Sau* Gruppen of JG300 was in question. After a heated argument between Luftwaffe commanders II/Sturm/JG300 and IV/Sturm/JG3, both equipped with heavily armed FW 190s, were returned to defence duties. In October '44 III/JG300, equipped with Me 109 night fighters, joined the rest of the Geschwader at Asbach. When the invasion of Europe was well established the bombers turned their attentions again to Germany.

Major Walter Dahl stayed with JG300 as Kommodore to prepare them for daylight operations before taking up the post of Inspector of Day Fighters in January '45. After 14 days of intensive training JG300 joined the *Reichsverteidigung* units.

On July 7th, 1944, the US 8th and 15th Air Forces launched a major attack aimed at the German aircraft industry and over central Germany a ferocious battle developed. 55 four engined bombers, *Viermot* to the fighter pilots, were brought down, but it marked the beginning of a struggle for survival for the Luftwaffe. This photo was taken just after the July 7th battle at Illesheim. Left: Lt. Oskar 'Ossi' Romm, (St.Kp. Sturmstaffel IV/JG3) Hptm. Wilhelm Moritz (Commandeur IV/JG3) and Major Dahl.

Major Dahl (right) with the officers of JG300.

The Gruppenstab of IV/Sturm/JG3 (Udet) as they taxi out from Schongau.

The commander of I Jagdkorps (in control of day defence fighter units) was Generalmajor Josef Schmid. Here he crosses a waterlogged field with JG300's Walter Dahl.

Hauptmann Wilhelm Moritz was awarded the Ritterkreuz on July 18th, 1944, after bringing down 41 aircraft. Moritz had made a name for himself as Kommandeur IV/Sturm/JG3 from April '44. In November he was forced to give up his command due to total exhaustion and took the less demanding post of Kommandeur IV/Erg.JG1.

I/JG300 flew Me 109Gs as high altitude protection to Sturm units. Their job was to give the other fighters a clear run into the bomber formations and take on any escort fighters. The Gruppenkommandeur was Hauptmann Gerhard Stamp, who had been awarded the Ritterkreuz for his work as a bomber pilot.

Taking a rest at Schongau are, left, Leutnant Romm, and centre, Moritz.

Stamp went on from JG300 to head a special Me 262 unit in November '44.

The Sturmstaffel of JG1 under Major Kornatzki was, like the other Sturm units, charged with the dangerous task of attacking the heavy bombers. Other units would attempt to hold the escorts at bay. One of the most daring Sturm pilots was Willi Maximowitz, who first flew with JG1, then in the summer of '44 with 10 and 11 Staffel JG3. He brought down 25 aircraft, 15 of them bombers. Of these Willi destroyed no less than 7 by ramming. For his efforts he was awarded the Deutsches Kreuz in Gold, but was killed on April 20th, 1945, aged 25.

Adolf Galland, General der Jagdflieger, and Oberst Trautloft, Inspector of Day Fighters, visit JG26 on the Western Front in the summer of '44. Here they are in conversation with 'Pips' Priller (left). Priller brought down his 100th aircraft, a B-24 Liberator, on June 15th, 1944, and was awarded the Swords to his Ritterkreuz on July 2nd.

An Oberst speaks with JG26 pilots. Priller is on the right in peaked cap and life jacket.

Come rain or shine the continuous operations went on. An FW 190 of 3/JG26 kicks up the dust amidst the summer blooms.

Leutnant Kurt Wiegand makes his report to Priller, on the bike, after returning from a sortie. Of Wiegand's 32 victories, 7 were against four engined bombers.

Hauptmann Diethelm von Eichel-Streiber took over command of I/JG27 in August '44. Von Eichel-Streiber had been Kommandeur III/JG51 (Mölders) in Russia and brought down 71 aircraft. He received the Ritterkreuz on April 5th, 1944, and finished the war flying Me 262s with JV44.

Despite all their efforts and sacrifices the Luftwaffe could not halt the progress of the American daylight bomber offensive. Steeled on by the knowlege that the bombers were carrying their bomb loads to the towns of Germany the fighter pilots fought with incredible courage and determination. These B-17s are from the 95th Bomb Group, which flew 320 missions and lost 157 planes during the war.

'Texas Chubby' of the 91st Bomb Group.

'Poop Deck Daddy' a B-24 Liberator of the 392nd Bomb Group based at Wendling, Norfolk.

On August 17th, 1943, the V weapon development establishment at Peenemünde/East was heavily damaged in an air raid. Development work on the Me 163 at Peenemünde/West was not affected and the following month Erprobungskommando 16 was formed at Zwischenahn, near Oldenburg, under the command of Hauptmann Späte. The new Kommando had an establishment of 150 men, 5 instructors and 23 pupils. As training progressed there were many accidents as the students tried to get to grips with the idiosyncrasies of the tiny fighter, but all the time more valuable knowledge was being gained.

On December 30th, 1943, Ritterkreuz holder Josef Pöhs was killed when the jettisonable undercarriage of his Me 163 bounced back off the runway and hit the plane. In January '44 the first fully operational variant, the Me 163 B-V14 arrived at Bab Zwischenahn, and in February Hauptmann Olejnik took command of 1/JG400. On March 1st, men and machines moved to Wittmundhafen to begin operations. The following month 2/JG400 was formed at Oranienburg under the command of Hauptmann Böhner.

The development of the rocket fighter. The Me 163 V-3 development machine and in front of this the Me 163B. Photographed at Bad Zwischenahn.

Front view of the Me 163B-1 showing the fitting of the two MK108 30 mm cannon.

The rocket fighter, below with power on and above returning to earth as a glider. Flying the 163 called for exceptional courage and skill.

The Me 163B-V7 is transported on a special trailer and lifted by air bags to prevent damage to its structure.

Caution was needed when filling the two fuel tanks. Here 'C' Stoff is pumped in, next to this was the 'T' Stoff tank. 'C' Stoff was a 30% hydrazine hydrate solution in methanol, while 'T' Stoff was 80% hydrogen peroxide plus a stabilizer. 'T' Stoff could only be kept in aluminium containers, steel would disintegrate, and anything organic would spontaneously combust. If pilot or ground crew ever came into contact with this they would die a most horrific death. The 'C' Stoff could only be held in glass, enamel or anodised tanks, and corroded aluminium. When the two met, in even the most minute quantity, an explosion was instantaneous.

The Me 163B-V14 one of the prototypes for the operational B series.

Everyday scenes at Bad Zwischenahn, home of Erprobungskommando 16. A 163 makes a 'Hot Start'.

The Me 163 had a performance the like of which had never been seen. The initial rate of climb was 3,600m/min. rising to 10,200m/min. at 10,000m. To reach its service ceiling of 12,100 metres took 3.35 minutes.

There was only sufficient fuel for a maximum of 8 minutes, around 6 under operational conditions at full power, after which a landing had to be made unpowered and on the skid. On the airfield the 163s were moved on specially built *Scheuschlepper* tractors.

Unteroffizier Rolf Glogner (right) dons the special overalls as the mechanic is wearing. These were made of Asbestos-Mipolamfibre, supposedly impervious to the fuel, but tragically more than one man found out that they did not always work.

The first production Me 163B-1as were delivered to Erprobungskommando 16 in July '44.

Leutnant Fritz Kelb flew both the Me 163 and Me 262, scoring victories with both. He died in an Me 262 crash when flying with JG7 on April 30th, 1944.

It would only take a small fuel leak to cause a disaster, for this reason it was not recommended practice to land with any fuel left in the tanks. To prove that a pilot could bale out safely Fritz Kelb volunteered for this experiment, and survived.

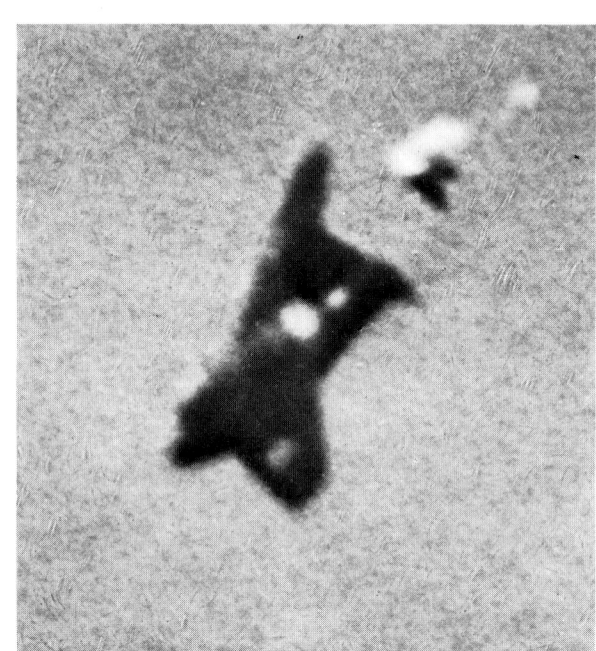

24 year old Ritterkreuz holder Oberleutnent Kurt Ebener had scored 33 victories with II/JG3 in Russia and then became an instructor before being posted as Staffelkapitän to 5/JG11. He was shot down over the invasion front and severely injured on August 23rd, 1944, and taken prisoner by American forces.

III/JG53 flew from the Stuttgart area in September '44. Here the Gruppen Kommandeur, Major Franz Götz, takes off. Götz had flown with the Gruppe since 1940, but was promoted to Kommodore JG26 on January 28th, 1945. He brought down 63 aircraft, 5 of which were four engined bombers.

Gerhard Michalski was also a successful pilot with JG53 and went on to become Kommodore of JG4 in August '44. He was promoted to Major on November 25th, and received the Oak Leaves to his Ritterkreuz. 13 of his 73 victories were against *Viermots*. This photo was taken when Michalski was a Staffelkapitän in II/JG53 in the Mediterranean.

117

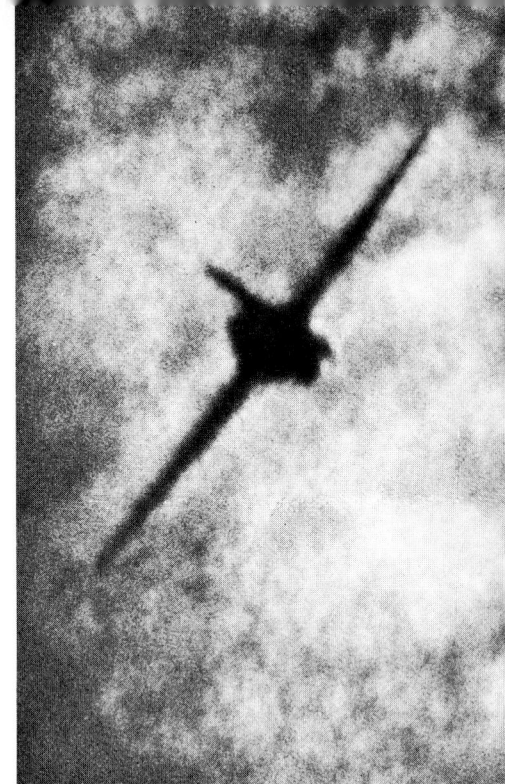

An everyday scene over the heart of Germany. The two larger trails indicate the path of Me 163s.

The pilots trained at Bad Zwischenahn went on to form two operational units. The first of these was 1/JG400 under Hauptmann Olejnik at Wittmundhafen. In July they received their first Me 163s and then moved to Brandis, near Leipzig.

On July 28th, American crews saw the rocket fighter for the first time when escorting P-51 pilots of the 359th Fighter Group saw five of them. It is believed that only 9 victories were claimed by Me 163 pilots, Feldwebel Siegfried Schubert claimed 3 of them. On one occasion he destroyed two B-17s, but crashed on take off from Brandis on October 7th, 1944, and as usual with a 163 crash he was killed.

2/JG400 formed at Venlo under Hauptmann Böner also went to Brandis and formed I/JG400 under Hauptmann Fulda.

Oberfeldwebel Reukauf of 2 Staffel takes a rest while waiting to scramble. 15 minutes after this photo was taken the order to scramble came, Reukauf began his take off procedure — and the Me 163 exploded, with its usual fatal results.

JAGDFLIEGERHEIM WIESSEE

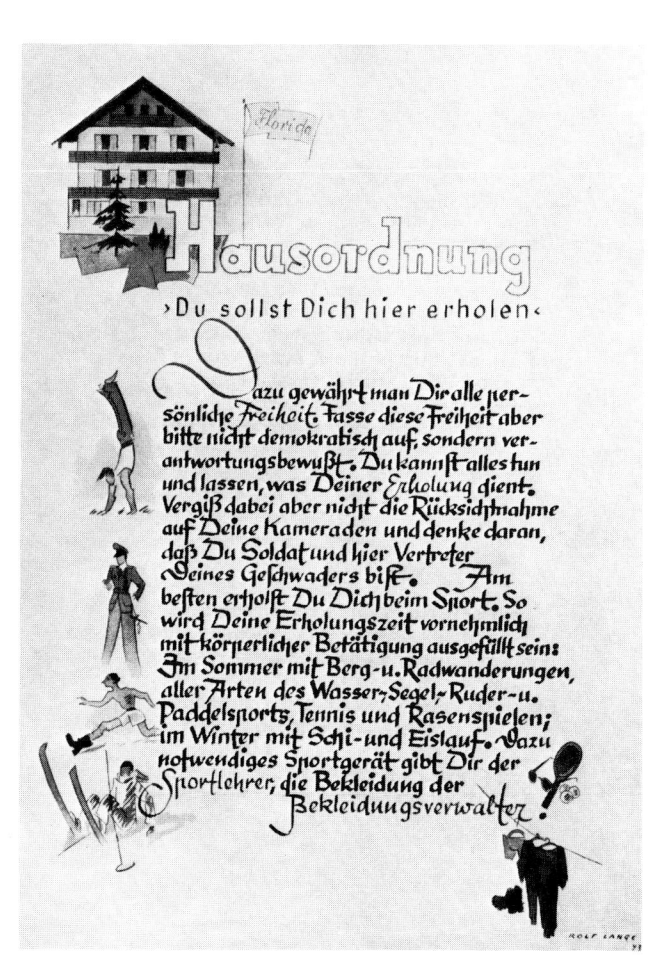

The bus to the Florida Hotel at Bad Wiessee. Many a fighter pilot spent his leave here, in what became known as 'Fighter Town'. Far from the pressures of daily combat the pilots could relax for a few precious days.

The house rules of 'Fighter Town' were drawn up by Rolf Lange, father of the last Kommodore of JG51 Dr Heinz Lange.

Both day and night fighter pilots spent their leaves in the summer of '44 at Tegernsee. Left, Hauptmann Augenstein (Staffelkapitän 12/NJG1) and right, Hauptmann Robert Weiss (Kommandeur III/JG54).

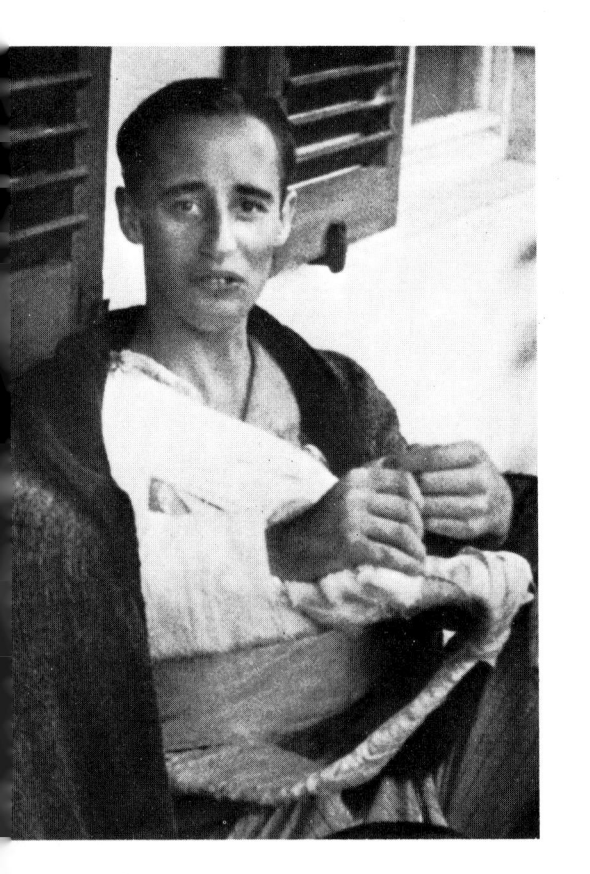

One of the popular forms of recreation was sailing, Hauptmann Walter Krupinski at the helm.

Oberleutnant Hans Weick, Staffelkapitän 10/JG3 was one of the most respected leaders in the defence of the Reich. In the late summer of '44 he was recuperating at 'Fighter Town' after being wounded.

This Me 109G-10 with 'Erla Haube' and pressurised cockpit was the mount of Leutnant 'Ossi' Romm in the late summer of '44. Romm led the high altitude staffel of JG3 whose purpose it was to protect the Sturmgruppen from fighter attack.

Galland welcomes some of the most accomplished home defence pilots: Left to right: Oberst Hannes Trautloft (Inspector of Day Fighters), General der Jagdflieger Galland, Major Kornatzki (Kommodore JG4) Hauptmann Krupinski (Kommandeur II/JG11) and Hauptman Albrecht (Kommandeur IV/JG53).

Hauptmann Karl Borris, Kommandeur I/JG26, at an American 0.5 inch machine gun.

September, 1944, was a black month for JG26. The bashful smile of Oak Leaves holder Hauptmann Emil 'Bully' Lang, an accomplished pilot with JG54 on the Russian Front. On June 29th, 1944, he became Kommandeur of II/JG26 on the Western Front. Here he brought down 25 aircraft, but on September 3rd, he was brought down by Thunderbolts near St. Trond and killed. His total number of victories stood at 173.

Another Ritterkreuz holder to come from JG54 was Leutnant Karl Kempf. He flew with 2/JG26 and, like Lang, was killed on September 3rd. His aircraft was shot down by Mustangs when taking off from Bael in Belgium. Of his 65 victories, 16 were in the West, at least two were *Viermots*.

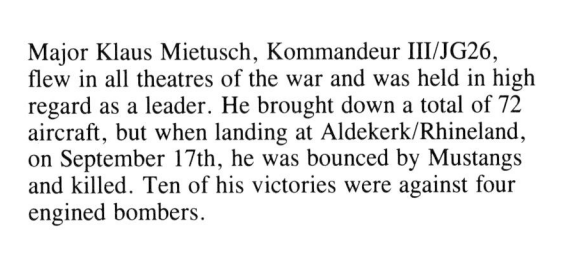

Major Klaus Mietusch, Kommandeur III/JG26, flew in all theatres of the war and was held in high regard as a leader. He brought down a total of 72 aircraft, but when landing at Aldekerk/Rhineland, on September 17th, he was bounced by Mustangs and killed. Ten of his victories were against four engined bombers.

September 27th was a hard day for the bomber attacking Sturmgruppe of IV/JG3. The Gruppe took off from Luchau, near Berlin, to intercept a large B-24 force attacking Kassel. 24 year old Feldwebel Willi Unger was one of the most successful pilots in the deadly art of bringing down the *Viermot*. He only engaged the enemy 34 times, but he brought down 22 aircraft, 19 of them heavy bombers, and was shot down himself on three occasions. On October 23rd he was promoted to Leutnant and awarded the Ritterkreuz.

Leutnant Oskar Romm, Staffelkapitän of 15/JG3, brought down three B-24s on September 27th. The following day he shot down two more *Viermots*. 'Ossi' Romm had received his Ritterkreuz on February 29th, 1944, after 76 victories with 1/JG52 on the Russian Front.

B-24 'Black Nan' goes down after a flak shell exploded near the port outer engine. This horrific photo was taken from an accompanying bomber as the wing and engine break off, instantly the 'plane has flipped onto its back. The engine has folded back on the top surface of the wing and the main wheel is sticking out of the wing in its retracted position. 'Black Nan' was from the 779th Sqn. 464th Bomb Group, 15th Air Force and the photo was taken over Northern Italy on April 9th, 1945. Only one man got out alive.

I and II/ZG26 re-equipped with Me 410s in the autumn of '43. It was hoped that the Me 410 would survive where its predecessor, the Me 110, had been so vulnerable. The new *Zerstörer* carried a formidable armament of 21 cm rockets, 20 mm and 7.92 mm forward armament and BK5 50 mm cannon. They were based at Königsberg/Neumark in East Prussia.

On February 22nd, 1944, II/ZG26 lost their Kommandeur, Major Eduard Tratt. Tratt had flown the Me 110 since 1940 and was the highest scoring *Zerstörer* pilot, with 38 victories, 25 of which were in the West in the air and 26 aircraft and 24 tanks destroyed on the ground. He was posthumously awarded the Oak Leaves to his Ritterkreuz on march 26th, 1944.

Left, the Me 410B-2/U2/R4 packed an incredible eight MG151 20 mm cannon and two MG17 7.92 machine guns in the nose. Right, an alternative armament were twin Wfr.Gr.21 rocket mortars. The third variant of the Me 410 (below) was the Umrüst-Bausatz 4, the reference given to the modification which fitted the 50 mm BK5 cannon. In all variants of the Me 410 there were two 13 mm MG131s in remotely controlled barbetts for defence.

In the hands of a determined and experienced pilot this was a formidable bomber destroyer, but how would it fare against the American escort fighters?
The answer was not long in coming. On May 13th, 1944, II/ZG26 were bounced by Mustangs escorting B-24s to Poznan. The losses were so high that the Gruppe was disbanded.

JG300 were now fully operational as day fighters. Feldwebel Wolfgang 'Lumpi' Hunsdorfer flew with 2 Staffel from Borkheide. The personal badge on his Me 109G-10 was a dog holding the inevitable *Viermot* in his teeth. 'Lumpi' was killed on March 29th, 1945.

I/JG300 scramble from Borkheide in September, 1944. Gruppenkommandeur at this time was Ritterkreuz holder Hauptmann Gerhard Stamp.

Oberstleutnant Walter Dahl, Kommodore of JG300, with his FW 190 in September '44 celebrating his 75th victory.

To keep pace with the tremendous losses, output from training units had to be maintained at a high level. High scoring fighter pilots lectured on tactics to the new generation, but there was no substitute for experience. Here Ritterkreuz holder Oberleutnant Karl-Heinz Bendert passes on the knowledge gained in 5/JG27 to students at Schul-Jagdgeschwader 104, Fürth/Bayern. Bendert had 54 victories, including 9 *Viermot*.

From April to September '44, Hauptmann Walter Nowotny was Kommodore of Schul-Jagdgeschwader 101 at Pau in Southern France. Nowotny had over 255 victories in Russia and held the Ritterkreuz with Oak Leaves, Swords and Diamonds. The aircraft used at Pau/North and South were a mixture of tandem seat Me 109G-12s and Dewoitine 520s.

The Dewoitine 520s had been captured from the French Air Force.

The standard advanced training aircraft for the Luftwaffe was the Arado Ar 96B. It was powered by an Argus As 410A-1 V-12 engine which gave it a maximum speed of 330 km/hr.

The production of fighters reached a high point in 1944, but it was too late to stem the rising tide of Allied bombing. Galland, as General der Jagdflieger, had petitioned the German High Command persistently for greater resources, but for months his requests fell on deaf ears.

Just as bomber production was changed in favour of fighters, so bomber crews were now being retrained as fighter pilots. Göring makes a visit to a group of ex-bomber pilots soon to be defending their homeland.

Oberst Hannes Trautloft, Inspector of Day Fighters, was also vociferous in his demands.

FW 190s of 9/JG301 at readiness. Like its sister unit JG300, JG301 were also converting from *Wilde Sau* night fighters to day defence duties.

An Me 109G-10/R6 prepares to take off from a makeshift runway amidst the bombed out buildings.

Farm land also served well for a few days or weeks. Nearby woods provided excellent camouflage from the ever present Allied reconnaissance and air strikes.

Flak divisions played a significant part in the *Reichsverteidigung*. Cities and major industrial areas and especially Berlin were ringed by Flak batteries. The guns were mostly 88 mm, but special bunkers were also built to mount twin 128 mm guns.

A direct hit from Flak was almost certain to blow a bomber apart. This was 'Wee Willi' 42-31333, the oldest B-17 of the 91st Bomb Group. 'Wee Willi' had completed over 120 missions before its dramatic demise on April 8th, 1945, and was the last B-17 to be lost in action by the 91st. Incredibly some of the crew, including the pilot l/Lt. Robert Fuller, managed to get out.

The operations room of II/JG300 at Löbnitz in the autumn of '44. Leutnant Klaus Bretschneider (left) was a successful *Wilde Sau* night fighter pilot, bringing down 14 aircraft in 20 sorties. He continued his success when his unit turned to daylight operations and on October 7th, 1944, he brought down 3 *Viermots* one of which he rammed.

Bretschneider (centre) with the unit medical officer Stabsarzt Felske (left) and his mechanic Obgerfreiter Schmidt.

Bretschneider was obviously hard on his aircraft, this is his 'Rauhbautz VII' which can be translated to 'Tough Guy'. He was awarded the Ritterkreuz on November 18th.

8/JG300 at Löbnitz was led by Leutnant Sprengst.

Unteroffizier Paul Lixfeld of 6/JG300 poses with his 'Yellow 12'. This rather well used machine is in the night finish used for nocturnal *Wilde Sau* operations and carries the Wild Boar itself on the cowl.

Schwarmfürer of 5/JG300 Unteroffizier Ernst Schroder was another who liked painting his mount. The inscription is a well known carnival shout from Cologne, and on the opposite side of his 'Red 19' the name 'Edelgard' was painted.

Constant Allied ground strafing forced Luftwaffe units more and more into cover. This is 6/JG300 appearing from the trees at Löbnitz.

Following Hitler's decision to adapt the Me 262 as a fast bomber a development unit was formed under the command of Major Wolfgang Schenk. In keeping with the Führer's directive, pilots from the bomber unit KG51 swapped their Ju 88s for the jet at Lechfeld. After four weeks training they left to begin operations against the invasion forces.

On October 4th, 1944, the fighter unit became operational from the airfields at Hesepe and Achmer, near Osnabrück. The unit was named after its highly decorated leader Walter Nowotny, the *Experten* of the Russian Front, who instilled much of his personal elan into what was known as 'Kommando Nowotny'. The first operation came on October 7th, when Leutnant Schall, Feldwebel Lennartz and Oberfahnrich Russel each brought down Liberators. Three more jets were attacked by Mustangs when taking off from Achmer and two were shot down.

One of the pilots who intercepted the Kommando Nowotny 262s on October 7th was American *Ace* l/Lt. Urban Drew of the 361st Fighter Group. He shot down one of the aircraft lost on that day.

'White 4' taxies out at Achmer. Note the unusual, and very effective, mottled camouflage on the tail, this was a peculiarity of Kommando Nowotny machines.

A rare sight, Me 262s line up at Achmer. This was taken in October '44 on a day when bad weather ruled out any chance of a surprise air attack, normally the aircraft would be dispersed and camouflaged.

23 year old Leutnant Seigfried Lemke took over as Kommandeur III/JG2 in July '44 and received the Ritterkreuz. Here Major Bühligen presents the award. By the end of the war Lemke had brought down 96 aircraft, includng 21 *Viermots*.

Another recipient of the Ritterkreuz was Hauptmann Julius Meimberg, Kommandeur II/JG53, seen here receiving the cross from General Hentschel at Rütesheim on October 24th, 1944.

Hauptmann Bruno Stolle was Staffelkapitän of 8/JG2 flying sorties against RAF anti U-Boat patrols when he was awarded his Ritterkreuz in July '43. He went on to become Kommandeur III/JG2, then spent 7 months as an instructor before taking command of 1/JG11 in October '44. He ended the war as Kommandeur of the development unit for the Ta 154 at Rechlin. He had 35 victories, includng 5 heavy bombers.

Oberfeldwebel Walter Loos was just 20 years old when he joined III/JG3, but went on to become one of the elite group of successful *Sturmjäger* pilots. He flew only 66 operational missions but destroyed 38 aircraft, 22 of which were *Viermots*. He made good use of his parachute for he was shot down nine times, received the Ritterkreuz and, unlike most of his comrades, survived the war.

The rotund Oberleutnant Herbert Schob, seen here riding the BMW, was one of the most successful *Zerstörer* pilots. He flew with II/ZG76 in defence of the Reich, shot down ten *Viermots* and was awarded the Ritterkreuz. He ended the war flying with JG300.

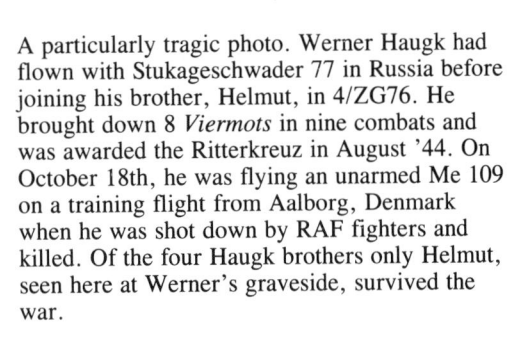

A particularly tragic photo. Werner Haugk had flown with Stukageschwader 77 in Russia before joining his brother, Helmut, in 4/ZG76. He brought down 8 *Viermots* in nine combats and was awarded the Ritterkreuz in August '44. On October 18th, he was flying an unarmed Me 109 on a training flight from Aalborg, Denmark when he was shot down by RAF fighters and killed. Of the four Haugk brothers only Helmut, seen here at Werner's graveside, survived the war.

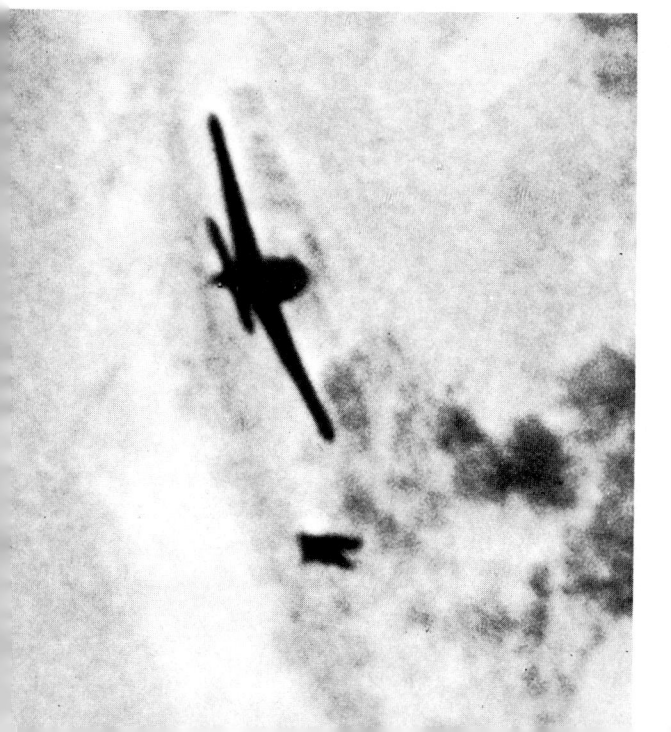

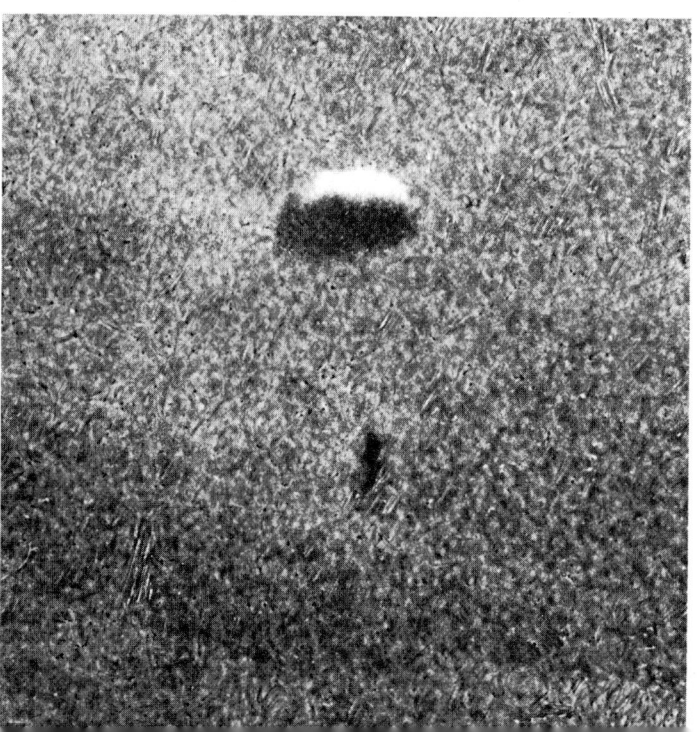

By late 1944, the Allies were winning the battle for air supremacy over Germany. This dramatic series of camera gun stills records the demise of an FW 190D-9.

By October '44, II, III, and IV Gruppe JG53 were based in the Stuttgart area at Heidelberg and Baden-Baden. Once more the safest place to hide was in the forest and taxi out to take off from a convenient field.

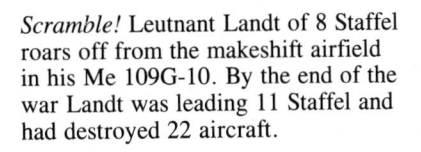

Scramble! Leutnant Landt of 8 Staffel roars off from the makeshift airfield in his Me 109G-10. By the end of the war Landt was leading 11 Staffel and had destroyed 22 aircraft.

By the late summer of '44 I and III Gruppen JG300 had moved to Borkheide, near Berlin. Here General Galland has just landed his heavily armed machine for an inspection. Left to right: Major Iro Ilk (Kommandeur III/JG300) Major Wittmer, Galland and Generalleutnant Schmid.

At the end of October, I/JG300 were caught by Mustangs in a surprise attack as they took off. Here the 109s burn fiercely in a scene repeated many times on Luftwaffe airfields in the last months of the war.

The Great Push

Despite Allied efforts to disrupt aircraft production the output still increased. On November 12th, 1944, General der Jagdflieger Galland announced that 3,700 aircraft of many different types had been built in readiness for *Der Grosse Schlag*.

The experienced fighter pilots were by now reaching the point of total exhaustion, only with difficulty could a sufficient force be gathered together for the Ardennes Offensive. All hopes were now pinned on a heavily armoured counter attack which would stop the Allied armies in their tracks, but it came to nothing. Prior to the launching of the counter attack Göring issued his Reichmarschall's order No. 7 to rally his men to the cause:

"Fighter pilots! In the coming months our army will fight a battle which will bring either victory or defeat. The Luftwaffe must not fail in its task.

Comrades! Now is that time. To be successful we must forge ourselves into a new fighter force which will turn the tide again. Stronger, bolder and more determined than ever before. Now we must prove to the workers of Germany that they have not laboured in vain.

The enemy must learn again that to invade the German Homeland will only lead to a crushing defeat.

Those suffering at home, our threatened industries and our economy shall breathe again and be safe in the knowledge that 'our fighters' are keeping watch over the skies.

Commanders! Lead your men against the enemy. When your men stagger under the strain, stagger with them. When they rejoice in victory, rejoice with them.

Fighter pilots! We count on you. The great task before us will signal the rebirth of a new and stronger Luftwaffe which will again become accustomed to victory. Fight like demons and believe in the final victory.

Be inspired with a new confidence in battle, then will the victory be ours."

On November 8th, 1944, one of the Luftwaffe's most venerated and highly decorated fighter pilots died. After bringing down a B-24, his 258th victory, Major Walter Nowotny was shot down in an Me 262. Reports of his final mission are confused, but in the light of recent research it would seem certain that he was shot down by a Mustang pilot after one of his Me 262's engines failed.

After a cermonial memorial service in Vienna, Major Nowotny was laid to rest in the city's central cemetery. Near the crash site at Epe, not far from the airfield of Achmer, a memorial was erected to the young Austrian pilot who had become a legend to the German people.

The day after Nowotny's death a cloud of depression hung over his old unit as they moved to Lechfield to form a new jet fighter unit. Oberst Steinhoff was instructed to form this new unit, JG7, from the remains of Kommando Nowotny, Erprobungskommando Lechfeld and a number of accomplished pilots from other units. Leutnant Franz Schall, the most successful pilot of the old Kommando, became Staffelkapitän of 10/JG7.

Oberfeldwebel Hermann Buchner, an extremely successful ground attack pilot with SG2 who had destroyed 46 Russian tanks, became one of the first pilots to join the new III/JG7.

Oberst Gordon M. Gollob visited JG400 at Brandis in the late autumn of '44. Gollob was attached to the staff of the armaments ministry in charge of the development of all jet aircraft.

Hauptmann Robert Olejnik, the 34 year old Kommandeur of I/JG400 (2nd from right), with his pilots at Brandis.

Full of confidence, but these young rocket men had one of the most dangerous jobs in the Luftwaffe.

Leutnant Klaus Bretschneider of 5/JG300 received the Ritterkreuz on November 18th, 1944, after 31 victories. On Christmas Eve his heavily armoured FW 190 A-8 *Sturmjäger* was shot down by Mustangs near Kassel and he was killed.

Feldwebel Konrad Bauer of 5/JG300 was awarded his Ritterkreuz on October 31st, 1944, after 34 victories. By the war's end 'Pitt' Bauer had been promoted to an Oberleutnant with at least 68 victories including 32 *Viermots*.

Ritterkreuz holder Hauptmann Robert Weiss became Kommandeur III/JG54 in July '44. On December 29th he was shot down over Lingen by Spitfires and killed. His total of victories stood at 121 and he was posthumously awarded the Oak Leaves in March '45.

The most successful pilot of JG27 was Oberfeldwebel Heinrich Bartels. He received the Ritterkreuz in November '42 after 45 victories. On December 23rd, 1944, his aircraft was shot down by Thunderbolts near Bonn, but his body was never found and he remains listed as missing. He had brought down 99 aircraft and had been nominated for the Oak Leaves.

Great things had been asked of the Luftwaffe in the Ardennes Offensive, but they had been unable to turn the tide against the Allies. The final all out strike was launched at dawn on New Year's Day, 1945, under the code name *Bodenplatte*. All available aircraft were to surprise the RAF fighters on their airfields in Northern France, Belgium, and Holland. To achieve this the fighters had to fly at low level over the German Flak belt which should have been ordered to cease fire. The command, however, came too late and the gunners unwittingly opened fire on their comrades. Losses were heavy, around 300 pilots, including 59 commanding officers, were killed or did not return that morning. Around 400 Allied aircraft were destroyed on the ground. This sketch appeared later in the wartime Luftwaffe magazine *Der Adler*.

As *Bodenplatte* took place over Allied occupied country no Me 262s were used in the attack. Instead II/KG51 stayed firmly on the ground at Hopsten/Rheine.

Oberst Trautloft and Major Andres (Kommodore EJG2) with III/JG7 at Lechfeld. Left to right: Major Eder, Major Hohagen (new Kommandeur of III/JG7), Major Andres, Oberst Trautloft and the chief instructor on the Me 262 with III/EJG2, Oberleutnant Wörner.

Although a two seat training version of the Me 262 was produced there were insufficient to fully equip the units.

Hauptmann Herbert Nölter received the Ritterkreuz in recognition for his work as a bomber pilot with I/KG3 in Russia. He took over command of III/JG300 and then II/JG301 which was being equipped with the new Ta 154. Nölter was shot down near Halberstadt in April '45 and was mortally wounded, succumbing to injuries on May 13th.

So critical had the fuel situation become in the last months of the war that none could be spared to taxi aircraft. At this school a twin seat FW 109 is towed past a surprised group of pupils.

Oberst Peltz, General der Kampflieger, pays a visit to his former bomber colleague Nötler's unit at Sachau and tries out one of the Ta 154s for size.

Although not reliant on conventional fuels there was none to spare for the special tractor units at JG400. Clearly only one ox is required to haul the diminutive Me 163.

Pilots of 2/JG400 await instructions to take off. Appropriately enough the badge adopted by the unit was a rocket powered flea. Although the number of victories scored by Me 163 pilots was insignificant, its effect upon the morale of Allied bomber crews was considerable.

'Red 13', the mount of Major Heinz Bär, Kommandeur III/EJG2. Bär, now holder of the Oak Leaves and Swords to his Ritterkreuz, ended the war flying with the elite JV44. His final total of victories stood at 220, 96 in Russia, 45 in North Africa, 21 *Viermots* and 16 when flying the Me 262.

The sleek lines of the Me 262 are shown to advantage here by 'White 13'.

Flaps down and undercarriage coming up, an Me 262 takes to the air.

In March '45 Hauptmann Erich Hartmann joined Major Bär at the Lechfeld school after his return from the Russian Front. Left to right: Major Hermann Staiger, Major Bär, Hauptmann Hartmann and Oberfeldwebel Leo Schuhmacher.

One of the few two seat Me 262s available to convert pilots onto the type.

Early in '45 the leadership of JG7 passed from Oberstleutnant Steinhoff to Major Weissenberger. Leadership of III Gruppe passed from Major Hohagen to Major Rudolf Sinner. Sinner, an experienced pilot with JG27 in North Africa, went to IV/JG54 in August '43 on the Russian Front. In February '44 he moved to III/JG54 in the west, but he was severely injured the following month. After his recovery he joined the training unit at Lechfeld as an instructor.

'Red 3' of JG7 taxies out with twin 21 cm rocket launchers under the fuselage, which are fitted with extended launching tubes.

Another JG7 machine with a starting trolley in foreground.

Continual reconnaissance sorties kept the Allies up to date with the movements of the Me 262 units. These missions were usually carried out at great height, out of range of ground defences.

Hauptmann Braunegg led the army cooperation photographic reconnaissance unit NAG6. They were equipped with Me 262s carrying two cameras in the nose.

In the final months of the war the Allies had gained total air superiority and roamed the skies over the Reich with impunity. Any German pilot taking to the air risked being attacked from the moment he taxied out to the moment he went into hiding again. Many an experienced pilot was lost at the vulnerable time of landing when any speed advantage was lost. To protect the jets at this time, conventional fighters flew defensive patrols over the airfields in an attempt to ward off Allied fighters.

Not only were aircraft the targets, but trains, vehicles and anything else that moved. Sadly it was not unknown for over zealous pilots to shoot at their victims as they parachuted to earth.

In a desperate attempt to solve the old problem of destroying American bombers without exposing fighters to their fire it was proposed that the BK5 50 mm cannon be fitted to the Me 262. Tests were not promising and the idea was shelved.

In factories hewn from the chalk hills near Vienna, and in the salt mines at Kahla/Thüringen, assembly of the Volksjäger got under way. From drawing board to maiden flight, the He 162 had taken only 69 days, but only 116 machines had been completed by the war's end. It had been proposed that the He 162 would be flown by boys from the Hitler Youth after receiving basic instruction in gliders, but it was fortunate for them that only I and II Gruppen JG1 were equipped with it.

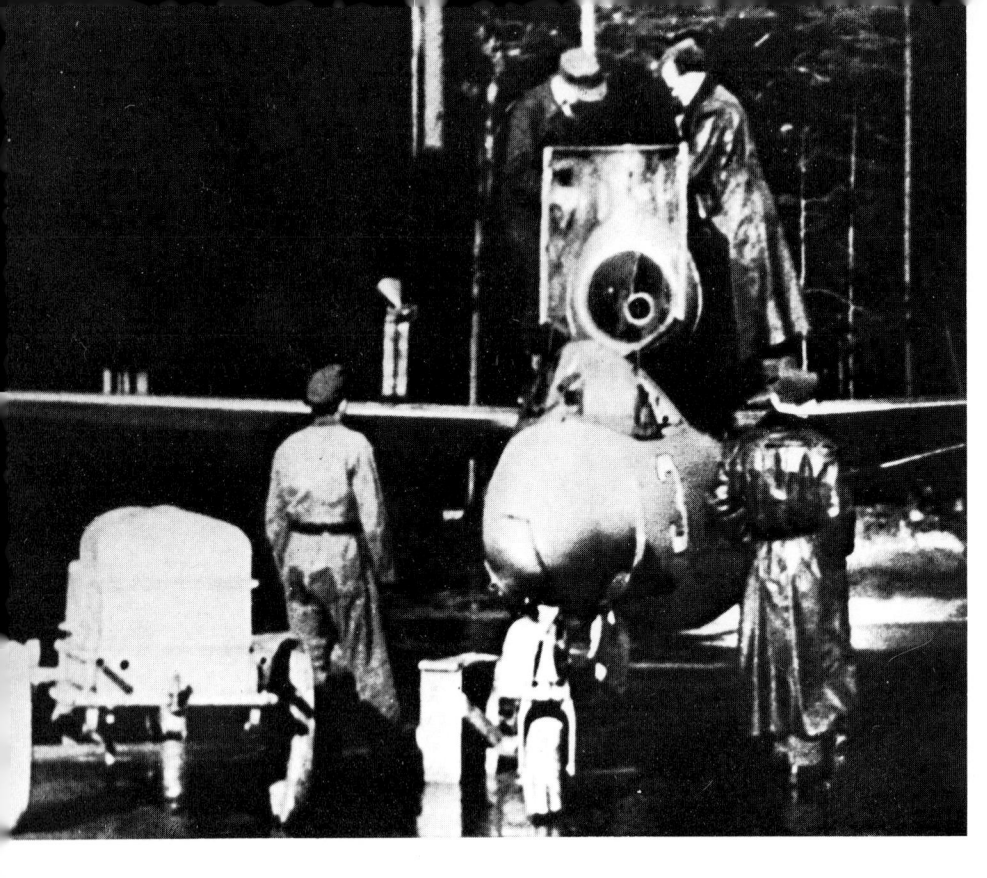

Mechanics work on the engine of a Volksjäger attached to the development unit Erprobungskommando He 162.

The battle had now become a desperate last ditch stand by the last few German fighter pilots. Here a B-17G of the 95th Bomb Group unhurriedly unloads its heavy calibre bombs.

24 year old Ritterkreuz holder Oberleutnant Wilhelm Hoffmann, the third of the one eyed fighter pilots, was shot down near Bissel/Oldenburg on March 26th, 1945. At the time of his death he was Staffelkapitän of 5/JG26 and had 44 victories to his credit including five *Viermots*.

IV/JG3 were equipped with the latest FW 190 development, the D-9, and were based at Prenzlau near Berlin. From here they flew fighter and fighter-bomber sorties under the leadership of Oskar 'Ossi' Romm, and Romm himself destroyed 6 aircraft while flying the D-9. On April 24th, 1945, the engine of Romm's D-9 overheated forcing him to crash land. He was seriously injured and spent the last days of the war in hospital. He had destroyed a total of 92 aircraft: 82 over Russia, 8 *Viermots* and 2 escort fighters.

Professor Kurt Tank's ultimate high altitude fighter was the Ta 152 H-1. It had an exceptional wing span of 14.82 metres, a pressurised cockpit and a Jumo 213 engine with 3 stage supercharger. By the war's end only 10 examples had been completed at the Cottbus factory.

Another variant of the Ta 152 was the short span heavily armed fighter designated the Ta 152 B-5/R11, but only a few prototypes were ever completed. Kurt Tank went on designing his aircraft to the last moment when British troops marched in and captured him on April 8th, 1945.

On March 18th, 1945, a new weapon was added to JG7's arsenal. This Me 262A-1b of 9/JG7 was one of the aircraft which attacked American bombers over Rathenow with 24 R4M rockets fired from beneath its wings. The rockets were launched from a range of 400 metres and 6 or 8 bombers were blown to pieces.

Twelve 55 mm R4M rockets were mounted beneath each wing on simple wooden rails and were released in a single volley. The R4M was developed by the Deutsche Waffen und Munitionsfabrik at Lübeck. After only a few weeks testing by Jagdgruppe 10 the rockets became operational.

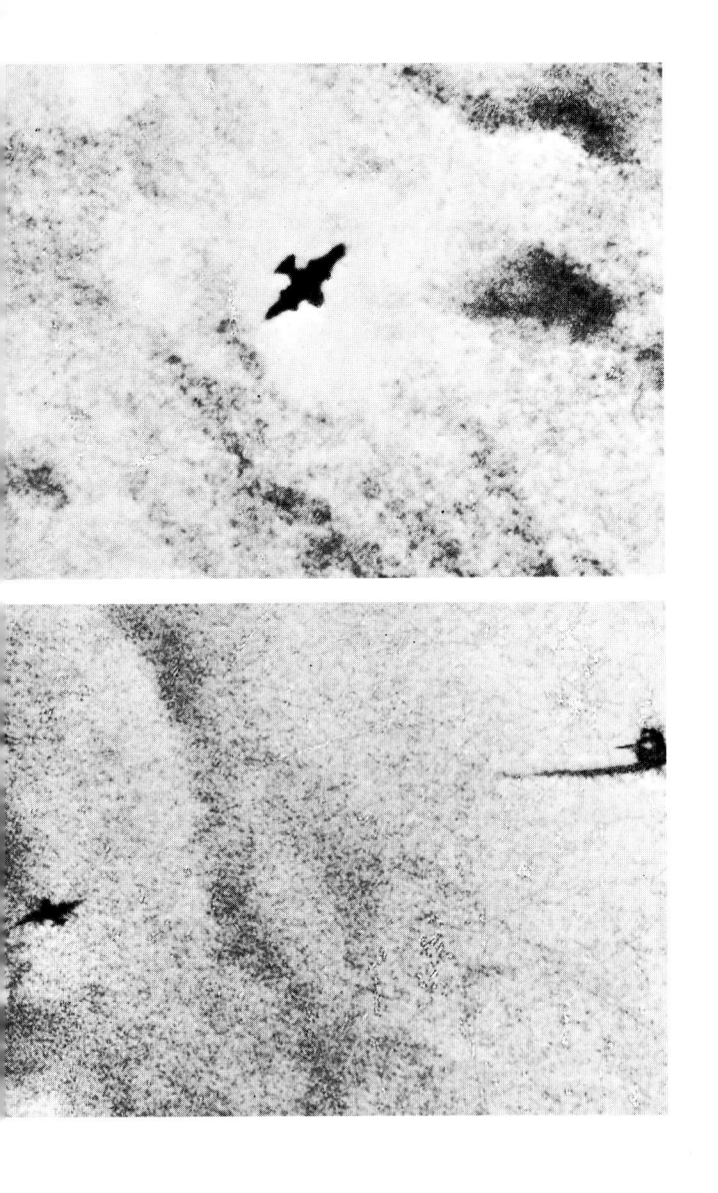

Four unique photos which captured the demise of Major Rudolf Sinner. They were taken by l/Lt Robert Crocker and Captain Kirke Everson over Parchim on April 4th, 1945.
1. Sinner's Me 262 dives into cloud. 2. Captain Everson's P-51 on Sinner's tail. 3. Closing on the Me 262. 4. The Me 262 crashes in flames, the white dot in the top left is Sinner's parachute.

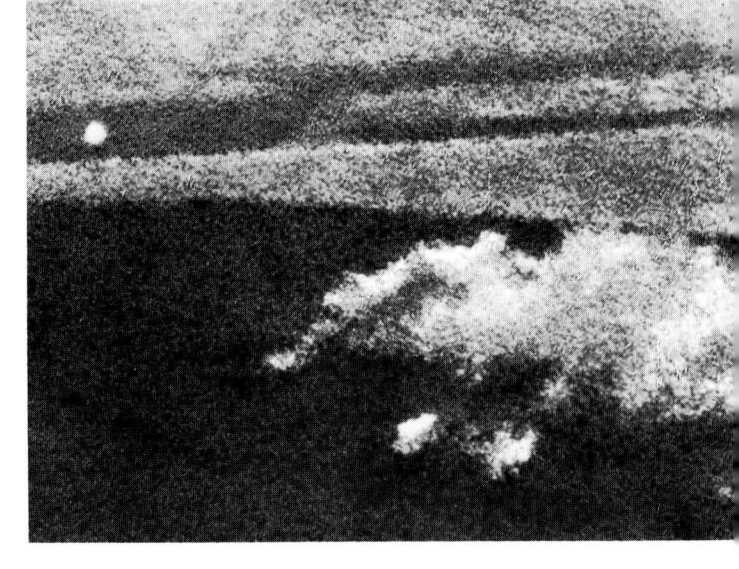

Copy

Sinner, Rudolf, Major   6.4.1945
Stab/III.J.G. 7 (Nowotny)

*Operations report for the mission of
4.4.1945*

On April 4th, I took off from Parchim to intercept a formation of enemy bombers. Enemy fighters were reported to be flying at 8,000 metres over the airfield, but this proved to be an over estimate. I circled at 400 metres under 8–9/10 cloud and after 1½ circuits joined up with 7 other aircraft to make up our formation. Climbing up through the cloud I saw 4 enemy aircraft flying in formation above me and against the sun (Thunderbolts). I climbed steeply but could not catch them, then one of the Thunderbolts dived steeply at me. I learnt later that these enemy aircraft were Mustangs. My rockets would not fire and the rest of the Gruppe had no luck.

I tried to out run the Mustangs, but saw 4 Mustangs behind me in an attacking position. I dived and turned sharply but was hit from behind and damaged. Then I tried a series of evasive manoeuvres but I could not throw off the Mustangs as I was now too low. I was now running from 8 Mustangs which were shooting at me. I tried to find some cloud cover in the hope of losing my attackers and attempted to fire my rockets but two of the Mustangs followed me closely. I did not see my rockets fire.

As I pressed the rocket firing switch my cockpit began to fill with dense smoke and I saw that my left wing was on fire. The fire soon reached the cockpit and I decided to bale out. The air speed was 700 Km/hr when I baled out, but I struck the tail in doing so. I realised that my parachute was not open and that my right leg had become entangled in the harness.

I was sure that my parachute had become detached from the harness, but when I found myself above the ground I grabbed the release handle and to my astonishment the 'chute opened with a bang. I performed about 3 somersaults as the 'chute opened and found myself hanging from the left strap only. The canopy did not develop fully and I landed heavily on my left leg and arm in a freshly ploughed field. I attempted to release the parachute harness but before I could do so I was dragged some 20 metres to a barbed wire fence which stopped me. Then two Mustangs strafed me as I lay on the ground. As the Mustangs circled I lay still, but when they moved away I dragged myself about 25 steps from my 'chute and hid in a deep plough furrow. Later I folded up the 'chute as it was attracting the enemy fire. Eventually the enemy were driven off by fire from Redlin (which I landed near).

I was given first aid by the crew of a Freya station and then treated by the medical officer of Jagdgruppe 10.

Sinner

One of the many projects reaching an advanced stage of development was the highly unconventional Do 335 *Pfeil* (Arrow). Professor Dr. Claudius Dornier patented the twin engined, centre line thrust configuration in 1937 and maintained an interest in the idea until a specification for a high speed interceptor was issued in 1942. The prototype Do 335V-1 made its maiden flight on October 26th, 1943 and was transferred to Rechlin for trials, while ten further prototypes were produced at Oberpfaffenhofen. In September '44 several of these machines moved to Erprobungskommando 335 which was to prepare the type for operations and develop tactics.

The *Pfeil* had the potential to be a tremendously powerful and fast fighter. The first production model, the Do 335A-1 attained 763 km/hr while the one-off Do 335A-4 reconnaissance aircraft reached 785 km/hr at 6,400 metres, it was the fastest machine in the series, and the fastest piston engined aircraft of the war.

When the Oberpfaffenhofen factory was overrun by American forces 11 Do 335A-1s and 2 tandem seat trainers had been completed, 15 more were nearing completion and 70 more were in various stages of assembly. There was also a B series, planned as the *Zerstörer*, but only 2 aircraft were flown, 6 more being found still under construction.

The following five photographs are stills from a cine film taken by a mechanic attached to 11/JG7 at Brandenburg-Briest on April 7th, 1945.

This home movie shows some of the every day scenes in the lives of the mechanics.

Several bomber units were equipped with the Me 262 in the closing stages of the war. To designate their new rôle the units added the letter J for Jäger to their identification as in KG(J) 51. Several Gruppen and Staffeln continued to operate from airstrips in Western Germany, such as Giebelstadt and Kitzingen, despite the heavy damage caused by American bombers on March 23rd.

One of the ex bomber units to convert to the Me 262 was KG(J)54, which was based at Neuburg/Donau. This is Oberfeldwebel Friedrich Gentsch, 7/KG(J)54, in the cockpit of his Me 262.

Hauptmann F. Wittkowsky, Gruppenadjutant of III/JG54, at Neuburg.

After the American raid of April 9th, there was little left of Neuburg. 155 B-17s of the 3rd Air Division dropped 421 tons of bombs, the hangars were smashed and the landing ground cratered, making it unusable.

In January '45 another new jet unit was formed at Brandenburg-Briest. At its head was Adolf Galland, now in disgrace in the eyes of Göring for siding with operational pilots rather than the Nazi commanders, who had been relieved of his post as General der Jagdflieger. Jagdverband 44 was formed from pilots of all ranks, but it is best remembered as the 'Ritterkreuz Geschwader' as it had ten Ritterkreuz holders in its ranks. The last move for JV44 took the unit to München-Riem from where the pilots flew some of the last operations of the war, it was one of the last outposts of the faithful Luftwaffe.

Three of the Luftwaffe's finest leaders talk in the courtyard of the converted girls school which acted as headquarters for JV44. Left to right: Oberst Freiherr von Maltzahn, Oberst Lützow and Oberst Trautloft.

Jets lined up at the edge of München-Riem.

Along the edge of the runways one man dug outs were made, into which pilots could throw themselves in the event of air attack. Even at this time there was still a little time for humour.

Oberst Johannes Steinhoff was Kommodore of JG7, but became the operations officer of JV44 and claimed six victories flying the Me 262. On April 18th he crashed on take off and was seriously burnt. In around 900 sorties he had destroyed 176 aircraft.

Oberstleutnant Heinz Bär was another high ranking officer who joined JV44. He arrived on April 23rd, 1945. Lt. Klaus Neumann (standing left), Lt. Leo Schuhmacher, OTL. Heinz Bär, Major Hohagen and right in the background Herbert Kaiser.

Left front, Major Krupinski, Major Brücker (Stuka pilot leader of Erpr. Kdo. Me 262 and General ground attack), Major Hohagen, OTL. Bär and at rear Leo Schuhmacher.

Leutnant Klaus Neumann (left) supervises the man-handling of his Me 262. Right is Leutnant Fährmann, Rottenflieger (wing man) to Steinhoff.

Oberst Lützow and Galland during their time with JV44. On April 24th, Lützow took off from Riem on what proved to be his last flight, for following a radio call which was believed to have come from the Donauwörth area he and his Me 262 went missing.

Two days after Lutzöw's death, Galland intercepted a Marauder formation in the Neuburg/Donau sector. He was then attacked by the Thunderbolt escort which crippled his Me 262, but Galland succeeded in bringing the fighter back to crash land between the bomb craters on the München-Riem airfield. Galland was taken to the Tegernsee hospital where he sat out the last days of the war.

After Galland had been wounded, Oberstleutnant Bär took over command of JV44, which had a strength of 60 operational aircraft, including those based at Salzburg and Innsbruck. On May 3rd, American tanks approached Salzburg where the last Me 262s were destroyed. The pilots began their long marches into captivity. Here Krupinski, Bär and Hohagen while away the last hours of their freedom.

At odd outposts all over Germany pilots awaited the moment when they would finally be captured, by the Americans or British if possible, as it was believed their treatment would be far preferable to that meted out by the Russians. Here Wolfgang Späte (Leader of JG7) and Major Gerhard Stamp (Sonderkommando 262) are deep in thought at Prag-Rusin.

Hauptmann Werner Wenzel (centre) of 9/JG7 with the rest of his pilots in a Bavarian forest in May, 1945.

In northern Germany, and especially at Leck, in Schleswig-Holstein, many units were overrun by the Allies. Aircraft were immobilised by taking off propellers and stripping out weapons. Pilots and ground crews were taken into captivity in their thousands.

Allied units discovered aircraft, wrecked and disabled, in every corner of the defeated Reich. Intelligence officers submitted reports on their finds and selected machines were brought to Britain and America for full evaluation.

I and II Gruppen JG1 began to receive the He 162 in April, '45 and were designated I/Einsatzgruppe JG1. Although they never became fully operational, Leutnant Schmidt claimed to have brought down a Typhoon on May 4th, the only known combat of the type. Top photo shows Oberst Herbert Ihlefeld, Kommodore JG1, with some of his pilots at Leck.

The conquering armies certainly found a few surprises. This is the Reichenburg IV, a piloted version of the V-1 flying bomb. It had been hastily prepared for suicide missions against key Allied targets in mid 1944 and a force of Selbstopfermanner (Self Sacrifice Men) had been recruited. They signed a form declaring 'I hereby voluntarily apply to be enrolled in the suicide group as a pilot of a flying bomb. I fully understand that employment in this manner will result in my own death.' The Re IV was never used.

One of the more spectacular developments of the Me 262 was the trial of a 50 mm BK5 cannon in Wn. 130083. This test bed was captured by the Americans and named Happy Hunter II, but it crashed on a ferry flight from Paris to Cherbourg. Test pilot Ludwig Hofmann, was killed in the crash.

This example was shipped to America for tests and survives in the Air Force Museum.

The Do 335 was the subject of great interest. An example being flown at Farnborough caught fire in the air and crashed on January 18th, 1946, killing Group Captain Hards, commanding officer of experimental flying at the Royal Aeronautical Establishment. Another one was preserved in America by the Smithsonian Institution and was returned to Germany in the 1980's to become the centre piece of the Deutsches museum in Munich.

Index

LUFTWAFFE UNITS

JG 1: 18, 19, 20, 21, 23, 26, 27, 38, 53, 64, 69, 77, 78, 83, 92, 94, 107, 161, 181.
JG 2: 17, 22, 34, 49, 53, 67, 69, 84, 97, 101, 141.
JG 3: 68, 84, 93, 104, 105, 107, 122, 123, 124, 125, 162.
JG 4: 57, 74, 117, 123.
JG 5: 97, 150.
JG 7: 68, 116, 148, 152, 158, 165, 167, 169, 178, 179.
JG 11: 27, 28, 29, 35, 39, 40, 41, 55, 60, 61, 66, 73, 74, 76, 82, 85, 96, 117, 123, 141.
JG 26: 22, 25, 30, 31, 34, 36, 39, 48, 63, 65, 68, 69, 75, 101, 108, 109, 117, 123, 124, 126, 162.
JG 27: 70, 80, 109, 150, 158.
JG 51: 109, 121, 126.
JG 52: 85.
JG 53: 76, 77, 89, 93, 101, 117, 123, 141, 144.
JG 54: 20, 34, 69, 122, 123, 124, 150, 158.
JG 76: 81, 86, 87, 88, 142.
JG 77: 25, 80.
JG 300: 82, 96, 103, 104, 105, 106, 129, 136, 137, 138, 145, 150.
JG 301: 96, 134, 153, 154.
JG 302: 96.
JG 400: 111, 119, 120, 149, 154, 155.
JV 44: 109, 173, 174, 175, 177, 178.
Eprg. Me 262: 98, 176.
Erpkdo. 16: 114, 115.
Erpkdo. 25: 27, 40, 43, 97.
Erpkdo. 162: 162.
EJG 1: 82.
EJG 2: 152, 156, 176.
Jagdgruppe 10: 43, 165.
Jagdgruppe 25: 56.
Jagdgruppe 50: 56.
KG 51: 139.
KG(J) 51: 152, 171.
KG(J) 54: 172.
Kommando Nowotny: 139, 140, 148.
Kommando Thierfelder: 98.
NAG 6: 159.
NJG 1: 122.
NJG 3: 59, 73, 82.
SJG 101: 131, 132.
SJG 104: 130.
ZG 26: 87, 99, 127.
ZG 76: 86, 87, 88.

GERMAN PERSONNEL

Albrecht: 123.
Anders: 152.
Augenstein: 123.
Bär Heinz: 83, 92, 156, 157, 176, 178.
Bartelmess: 41.
Bartels Heinrich: 150.
Bauer Konrad: 150.
Becker Ludwig: 24.
Beise: 23, 27.
Bendert Karl-Heinz: 130.
Bohland: 98.
Böhner: 111.
Borris Karl: 25, 31, 123.
Brauchitsch von: 74.
Braun Wernher von: 46, 102.
Braunegg: 159.
Bretschneider Klaus: 136, 137, 150.
Brücker: 176.
Buchner Hermann: 148.
Bühligen Kurt: 49, 67, 97, 141.
Christl Georg: 43, 74, 97.
Clausen Erwin: 40.
Dahl Walter: 95, 103, 104, 105, 129.
Dickfeld Adolf: 35.
Diesing: 74.
Diethelm: 109.
Dippel Heinz-Georg: 36.
Ebersberger Kurt: 36, 69.
Ebner Kurt: 117.
Eder Georg-Peter: 31.
Ehlers Hans: 64, 78.
Eichel-Streiber von: 109.
Fährmann: 176.
Falkenshamer: 28, 73.
Fest: 41.
Framm: 21.
Frank: 41.
Frey Hugo: 26, 35.
Fuhrmann: 73.
Galland Adolf: 35, 37, 43, 58, 63, 70, 71, 74, 80, 95, 97, 98, 108, 123, 133, 145, 177, 178.
Galland Wilhelm-Ferdinand: 36, 63.
Galland Paul: 63.
Geisshardt Friedrich: 25.
Gentsch Friedrich: 172.
Gerhard: 23, 26.
Geyer Horst: 37, 40, 43, 44, 74, 97, 100.
Glogner Rolf: 115.
Gollob Gordon: 149.
Goltzsch Kurz: 45.
Göring Hermann: 50, 71, 74, 133, 146.
Götz Franz: 117.
Grabmann: 82.
Graf Hermann: 56, 82, 85.
Hackl Anton: 66.
Handrik: 70.
Harder Jürgen: 76, 101.
Hardke: 43, 44, 45.
Hartmann Erich: 157.
Haugk Helmut: 87, 88, 142.
Haugk Werner: 142.
Hermichen Rolf: 39, 40.
Herrmann: 74.
Hofmann Ludwig: 182.
Hofmann Wilhelm: 48, 162.
Hohagen: 158, 176, 178.
Ibel: 95.
Ihlefeld Herbert: 56, 181.
Ilk Iro: 145.
Kelb Fritz: 116.
Kempf Karl: 124.
Koall: 31.
König Hans-Heinrich: 73, 96.
Kornatzki: 43, 74, 107, 123.
Kiel: 35.
Knoke Heinz: 20, 26, 28, 41.
Krupinski Walter: 122, 123, 176, 178.
Landt: 89, 93, 144.
Lang Emil: 124.
Lemke Siegfried: 141.
Lennartz Helmut: 41, 55, 99, 139.
Lent Helmut: 59, 82.
Lippisch Alexander: 102.
Lixfeld Paul: 138.
Loos Walter: 142.
Losigkeit: 18, 34.
Lützow Günther: 28, 29, 43, 44, 71, 174, 177.
Mader Anton: 27, 66.
Maltzahn Günther von: 71, 174.
Mayer Egon: 17, 53, 63, 69, 84.
Maximowitz Willi: 107.
Messerschmitt Willy: 32, 102.
Meimberg Julius: 141.
Michalski Gerhard: 117.
Mietusch Klaus: 101, 124.
Milch Erhard: 37, 40, 98, 102.
Mittelhuber Ludwig: 50.
Moritz Wilhelm: 104, 105, 106.
Müngerstorff: 67.
Münster Leopold: 93.
Naumann Johannes: 68.
Neumann Eduard: 43, 45, 70, 80.
Neumann Klaus: 176.
Nölter Herbert: 153, 154.
Nowotny Walter: 131, 139, 146.
Olejnik Robert: 18, 111, 149.
Oesau Walter: 17, 83, 92, 94.
Peltz: 154.
Petersen: 40, 98.
Perl: 35.
Philipp Hans: 69.
Pöhs Josef: 111.
Priller Josef: 34, 36, 63, 65, 75, 108, 109.
Recker: 99.
Reitsch Hanna: 102.
Reukauf: 120.
Riedel: 100.
Rollwage Herbert: 77.
Romm Ossi: 104, 106, 123, 126, 163.
Rosarius: 59.
Sanders Hans: 50.
Sauer: 92.
Schall Franz: 139, 148.
Schenk Wolfgang: 139.
Schmid Josef: 105, 145.
Schmoller-Haldry: 95.
Schmude: 26.
Schob Herbert: 142.
Schöfel: 22.
Schreiber: 99, 100.
Schröder Ernst: 138.
Schubert Siegfried: 119.
Schuhmacher Leo: 77, 92, 157, 176.
Schumann Heinz: 34.
Schwertfeger: 41.
Seiler: 34.
Siefert Johannes: 22, 34, 65, 75.
Sinner Rudolf: 158, 166, 167.
Sommer Gerhard: 66.
Späte Wolfgang: 111, 178.
Specht Günther: 35, 61, 66, 73, 82, 85.
Speer Albert: 40, 102.
Sprengst: 137.
Staiger Hermann: 157.
Stamp Gerhard: 106, 129, 178.
Steiger: 23.
Steinhoff Johannes: 148, 158, 175.
Stolle Bruno: 141.
Stumpf: 73.
Suss Ernst: 56.
Tank Kurt: 50, 51, 52, 164.
Thierfelder: 74, 98, 100.
Tratt Eduard: 127.
Trautloft Hannes: 43, 45, 74, 108, 123, 133, 152, 174.
Trockels: 41, 73.
Ubben Kurt: 80.
Unger Willi: 125.
Weik Hans: 122.
Weiss Robert: 123, 150.
Weissenberger Theodor: 97, 158.
Wendel Fritz: 32, 33, 37, 67.
Wenneckers: 55.
Wenzel Werner: 179.
Wiegand Gerd: 109.
Wilcke Wolf-Dietrich: 84.
Wittkowski: 172.
Wittmer: 145.
Woldenga: 80.
Wolf Albin: 21.
Wörner: 152.
Wurmheller Josef: 49, 101.
Zink: 41.